The Master Conversationalist:

Stories

Baker Hill

COPYRIGHT

Baker Hill Books

The Master Conversationalist

This book is a work of fiction. Everything and everyone is completely made up, especially Benedict Cumberbatch, Elon Musk, and Justin Timberlake. I made up these names. As far as I know, they are not real people. Any resemblance to actual persons living, dead, or anywhere in between is entirely coincidental.

Cover by @raycasso__

Baker Hill Books
Email me: bakerhillbooks@gmail.com
bakerhillbooks.com

First edition © 2021

DEDICATION

For Doc Rice

CONTENTS

THE BIG ORANGE GHOST

It is a sad but inevitable fact that everyone is eventually forgotten.

Except for you. You are the exception. Your descendants will sit around the Thanksgiving table two hundred years from now, passing around your college thesis.

So insightful!

And eloquent!

And they were only twenty-one when they wrote it!

But some people aren't so lucky. Some people invent the most influential thing in the history of humanity, and no one even remembers their name.

Some people are like me.

I was a prehistoric hominid from two-million B.C. And even though I was the greatest inventor the planet has ever seen, I'm willing to admit my accomplishment had nothing to do with talent. I was simply an ordinary man caught in one of the past's many riptides of fate. But whether or not I deserve credit for my role in the future of civilization is irrelevant. All that matters is that I was the particular bipedal ape whom destiny chose to change the world forever.

***

It all started when my wife, Brenda, and I were on our way to a dinner party at my brother, Bobo's, cave.

"Grog, we're slowing down," Brenda said. I pretended not to hear, but it was hard to feign momentary deafness when Brenda was seated directly behind me on the back of our elderly woolly mammoth, Phil.

For a moment, all that could be heard in the valley was Phil's blundering steps.

Then Brenda started poking me in the sides. "Did you hear me?" she said. "Phil's knees are about to buckle."

"He's just catching his second wind," I said. "In between gallops." But I knew better. Phil was a seventy-year-old woolly with a long gray beard below his trunk. Every time Phil took a heaving, wheezing step, I could hear the beast's lungs purring with phlegm. It was only a matter of time before Phil face-planted into the ground tusks-first, propping up his body for the valley's wildlife to attack his corpse from all angles. "We're almost at Bobo's cave anyway," I said. "I can nearly see it."

Brenda withdrew her hands from my sides and folded her arms. "Then we might as well walk from here."

I gritted my teeth. I could already see several young, luxuriously coated woolly mammoths coming into view on the horizon. They were parked outside a very large fancy cave with a humongous engraving above its stone door.

SABER CLAN, the engraving read. It must have cost a fortune.

I imagined the look on Bobo's face if he saw Brenda and I show up to his cave on foot. "We are not walking," I said.

Brenda groaned.

Phil wheezed.

And Bobo's cave drew closer.

***

I was tying Phil to an acacia tree outside of Bobo's cave when Bobo himself came outside. Bobo's magnificent saber tooth tiger robe slid down his shoulder a little as he stretched out his arms for a hug.

"Bring it in, little brother," Bobo began, but he cut himself off as soon as he caught sight of Phil. "My god," he said, stepping lightly toward my woolly. "What the hell is that?"

I looked up at Phil, who at the moment resembled a punch-drunk boxer trying to pull himself together for the twelfth round. Phil's tongue hung out of his mouth, dripping spit onto the driveway.

"It's our woolly, Phil," I said, trying to be nonchalant. "He brought us here."

Bobo shook his head in disbelief as he cautiously approached Phil. "I've never seen one this old."

I tried to nod, but I couldn't quite convert my wince into the right head movement.

Bobo looked over his shoulder at me. "Did you say you rode it here?"

"Yeah."

"So it can actually walk?"

I clenched my fists by my sides. "Are you surprised?"

"Surprised?" Bobo said, looking back up at Phil with awe. "I've never in my life seen a woolly mammoth with a wizard's beard."

At that moment, Bobo's wife, Katherine, came out of the cave with bear claw bracelets jangling from her open arms. "Hello, hello—" she stopped in her tracks when she saw Phil. "Oh my god. What is that?"

"It's their woolly mammoth," Bobo said. "They rode it here."

"No," Katherine said. She briefly glanced at one of her prized woollys as if she hoped she had misheard, and Brenda and I had actually ridden in on a much younger, healthier woolly who was much less prone to breaking down on the ride over. "No, no, no. You did not ride that old thing to my cave."

"Phil's actually a very reliable woolly," Brenda said.

Katherine turned to her as if noticing her for the first time. "Oh hello!" Katherine said. She gave Brenda a hug and plucked at one of her toga straps. "Oh this is so cute."

"Thank you."

"You tried to dress up for us." Katherine turned back to me. "Anyway, we'll lend you one of our woollys. It is simply not safe for you to ride back home on that ancient creature. You'll get halfway home and that thing will keel over and die on you. No, no, no. I will not let you both get eaten by an enteledon."

"He's a good woolly," I said.

"Nonsense," Katherine said. She gestured up at one of the strapping woolly mammoths next to her. "You'll take Bruno home."

"Helluva animal," Bobo said.

I tried to protest, but Katherine was already leading me and Brenda into the cave by our hands.

"Just wait until you see our new chandelier," Katherine said. "It's a treasure."

***

The chandelier was a saber tooth tiger rib cage suspended from the ceiling. "It's big," I said.

Bobo chuckled. "He's the biggest one anyone's ever caught in this valley by about forty pounds. Took me almost thirty rocks to kill him. Big rocks. Nice rocks too. The nicest." Bobo took a big shiny rock out of his toga and handed it to me. "I want you to have this."

"Oh," I said, looking down at the polished stone.

"It's the rock that finally killed the chandelier above you."

"How thoughtful," I said. I discreetly set the shiny rock down on Bobo's fifty-foot-long granite countertop.

"Anyway," Bobo said, "let's go drink its blood on the porch." But before we could reach the back door, two perfect little cave children came running down the steps.

"Mommy!" said the girl. "Can we take Bruno to the pond to throw rocks at birds?"

"Not Bruno," Katherine said. "Your uncle Grog and aunt Brenda's woolly mammoth is about a second away from dying, so they're going to need Bruno to get home."

"That's okay!" said the boy. "We'll take William."

"Hmm," Katherine said. "I think William's a little tired from our trip to our vacation cave by the lake. How about you take Henry or Lola?"

"Sounds like a good compromise!" said the girl.

"Great, now run along," Katherine said. "Ugh," she said to Brenda as she watched the kids turn the corner. "Don't you love perfect children? I can't wait for you two to be able to afford to have kids someday!"

***

I set the stone cup full of blood down on the table and sat back in my adirondack chair. We were out on Bobo's back patio, looking out at his expansive field of animal skeletons.

"How do you like the blood?" Bobo said.

"It's good," I said.

Bobo nodded and took another sip. "It requires a pretty sophisticated palette to appreciate." He set his stone cup down next to mine on the table and folded his fingers against his stomach. "Grog, I wanted to talk to you, little brother."

Here we go again, I thought.

"What do you think about working for me as a saber tooth tiger hunter?"

I took a deep breath before reciting the response I had uttered a dozen times in the mirror: "Brenda and I are quite content picking berries, Bobo."

"Right, the berries," Bobo said. He took another swig of blood. "You must be learning so much about what makes a woman tick."

I grimaced. "There are actually lots of men who pick berries."

"Right, like who?"

"Stan."

"I'm not familiar with Stan."

"He picks berries."

"Of course he does." Bobo took another sip of blood and looked contemplatively at some dusty rib bones sticking up out of the ground in the distance. "Then again, if you ever became interested in owning a big cave like this, a nice woolly mammoth, perfect children," he shrugged, "you might feel differently about throwing rocks at saber tooth tigers."

I swiveled in my adirondack chair. "Did you ever think that the reason why woolly mammoths are so expensive is because there are hardly any of them left? Hmm? And why is that, Bobo? Could it have something to do with the fact that you and your boys threw too many rocks at them?" I hadn't planned on going on the attack, but I had to admit, it felt good.

Bobo blinked at me.

"You're going to do the same thing to saber tooth tigers," I said. "It's not sustainable."

Bobo grinned. "Right. And that's why you don't throw rocks at animals. Because it's not sustainable."

"And because it's barbaric!" I shouted. Before I could get a hold of myself, I grabbed my chalice of blood and tossed it into the dirt in front of us.

Bobo stared at the red mud. "I just want to give you a good life, brother," he said. "Because right now, your life pretty much sucks."

I stood up.

"Where are you going?" Bobo said.

"I have an early morning tomorrow."

"But we were just about to bring out the tiger!"

I paused in the doorway. "Then I left right on time." I threw open the back door to the cave and found Katherine showing Brenda a stone tablet album of cave drawings.

"This one is Joey winning first place at the killing bee," Katherine said. "He killed a bird with an arrow."

"Brenda, we're leaving," I said and took her hand.

"What, why?" Katherine said.

"We have an early morning," I said on our way to the door.

Bobo was in fast pursuit. "Come on, Grog, you have to try the tiger!" He caught my arm at the front door. "It might make you change your mind."

I tugged my arm back. "I will never change my mind," I said, and as soon as Brenda and I were outside, I pushed the big, expensive stone slab door until it covered the entrance to the cave.

I was exhausted, but I felt light on my feet as I led Brenda toward Phil, who was sleeping soundly in the driveway.

"What was that all about?" Brenda said.

"I'll explain on the ride back," I said. "But for now, all you need to know is that you will never have to go to another dinner party with Bobo and Katherine again." My voice was almost giddy. I waited for Brenda to giggle or say What with so much glee, it would sound as if she just might burst. But instead, she stayed silent.

As soon as we reached Phil, I understood why. Phil had collapsed on the ground. His tongue hung out of the side of his mouth, resting on the dirt driveway. His lips were turning blue.

"I think he's dead," Brenda said, looking down at Phil's motionless body.

I put my finger next to Phil's cold neck but felt nothing. I waited for my beloved woolly to wheeze.

"Grog," Brenda said. She was looking back at Bobo's cave.

I knew what she was suggesting, but I wouldn't consider it; I couldn't even bear the thought. I continued frantically searching Phil's hairy neck for a pulse.

"Grog, I think we need to ask Bobo for help," Brenda said.

I pressed my fingers deeper and deeper into Phil's esophagus until his vertebrae poked against my fingertips. Still, not even a whisper of a heartbeat. My shoulders slumped. "Okay," I said, and patted Phil's head for the last time. "Okay."

***

The stars and moon were out on the ride home. I could see the whole valley. On any other night, I would have enjoyed the view, but on that night, I stared straight ahead the whole ride home. I tried my best not to think about how much smoother of a ride Bruno provided, and how Bruno's well-groomed fur underneath me didn't chafe my legs nearly as much as Phil's. But Brenda's silence meant there was little to distract me from the whir of my own ruminations. This silence promptly ended when we reached our cave.

"Grog," Brenda said softly as she dismounted from Bruno's obnoxiously roomy and luxurious backside.

"Yes?" I said. I was already on the ground, tying up our borrowed beast to the stake by our front door.

Brenda looked down at the ground. "I don't mean to upset you, but," she looked up at me hopefully, "do you think Bobo might be right?"

My fist tightened around Bruno's expensive leather reins. "Right about what?"

Brenda sighed. "About hunting saber tooth tigers."

My heart felt as if it had been stabbed by a wildebeest's horn.

"And listen," she said, "before you say it's barbaric and unsustainable and ruining the environment and everything else… I already agree." Her eyes were watering. "But…" She looked at our tiny cave, at the misshapen stone door that only covered half of the opening, the door that let in an ungodly amount of light in at sunrise.

"But what?" I said.

She wiped her eyes with her old toga. "I think it could really help us. Even if we just joined the profession for a little while. And then, we could go right back to picking blackberries. I promise."

To my surprise, for a moment her little fantasy became my own. I thought about all we could do with that saber tooth tiger money. Fix up our cave. Buy a new woolly. Maybe take a trip to the other side of the hill every once in a while.

I leaned in toward Brenda until our lips were only an inch apart, and looked into her eyes. "I will never ever participate in the murder of innocent animals," I said, and brushed past her.

She grabbed my arm. "I understand, Grog," she said. She reached into her pocket and pulled out a big shiny object and handed it to me.

"What's this?" I said, turning it over in my hand.

"It's the rock that Bobo used to kill their chandelier," Brenda said. She patted the rock. "Just in case you change your mind." Then, she clutched her ratty, torn toga, and headed into our cave. I heard her let out a strenuous grunt as she slid our front door shut.

I squeezed the rock in my hand and looked up at the stars.

Why? I thought. Why did I live in this world? Why couldn't I live in a world where everyone ate fruits and vegetables? It wasn't hard for me to imagine such a world. Instead of drinking blood and staring at a field of bones, everyone could sit in their adirondack chairs on their patios and watch the animals dance in their yards. And, sure, some of the animals would murder the smaller ones, of course, but let the animals do that.

But I wasn't born into that world. I was born into this one. This evil, unjust, carnivorous one.

My hand tightened its grip around the large, shiny stone in my toga pocket. In an instant, I realized I could no longer stand to hold it and everything it represented. I took it out of my pocket and chucked it as hard as I could against my cave wall.

Bruno, who was chewing grass, didn't look up as the rock collided against the wall with a loud crack. He didn't seem to notice the glint of light that shot out of the wall, nor the puffy gray cloud it started forming in the patch of dry grass underneath him. Even when the first tiny sprouts of red and yellow light burst out of the grass, Bruno continued to chew, completely undisturbed by the light growing larger, brighter, and hotter as it consumed the fringes of his grassy snack. The light was orange now, and dancing.

It looked like a big orange ghost.

The big orange ghost latched onto the tip of Bruno's snout, spread its ghoulish heat up his furry trunk, and wrapped his head in its warm, demonic embrace. Within seconds, the big orange ghost covered his entire body. Bruno took off running into our neighbor Klonch's yard, where the big orange ghost spilled out into the entire pasture, and spread to the fur of Klonch's twelve woolly mammoths, burning their bodies with the heat of a thousand suns. They ran around screaming in Klonch's yard. It was bright now. Bright like day.

I ran.

***

I don't remember entering my cave, only the feeling of cold sweat down the back of my neck as I struggled to close my front door behind me.

"What was that?" Brenda said. I could barely see her at the edge of the cave, sitting up in our dirt bed.

"Nothing," I said, and climbed into bed next to her.

"It sounds like screaming."

I pulled our hemp blanket over my shoulder and lay my head against the ground. "Screaming?"

She was still sitting up straight. "Yes, screaming. And it's bright outside. Is it morning?" She said, looking at the flickering light streaming through the gap in our cave door.

"Don't be ridiculous," I said. "Were you dreaming? It is night. Early night. The stars are out."

Outside, one of the woollys let out a chilling scream before it collapsed to the ground with a thud that shook our cave.

"What was that?" Brenda said. "And what is that crackling sound? And why is it so hot?" She thrust the blanket to the side and started climbing to her feet. I grabbed her hand.

"Brenda," I said. There was no use hiding anymore. My throat tightened as I thought of how I would explain to her that I had thrown a rock that created a glint of light against the cave wall that summoned a demon that killed Bruno, and the only way we were going to be able to pay Bobo and Klonch back for their woollys was if I enlisted myself as Bobo's indentured servant and hunted saber tooth tigers for the rest of my life.

Before I could begin, I heard a knock on my door. I jumped at the opportunity to delay my explanation to Brenda a little further, and ran to answer the door. When I opened it, I found a small, middle-aged, balding man in the cheap, plaid toga suit of a woolly salesman.

"Klonch?" I said.

My neighbor Klonch raised his hand, and at first, I thought he was going to hit me, but then I saw what looked like a very large turkey drumstick in his hand. But it wasn't a turkey drumstick. Turkeys didn't have fur.

"Taste it," Klonch said, offering me the woolly meat. He looked strangely sad.

"I don't eat meat," I said. I examined the meat. The big orange ghost had blackened the meat's edges with its heat-inflicting spells.

Klonch's eyes started to water. To my surprise, I realized that he was crying tears of joy. "What do you call it?" he said. "The thing that did this."

I looked down at the chunk of meat, then over Klonch's shoulder at the demon consuming his yard.

"The Big Orange Ghost," I said.

***

I have summoned a demon before.

When Bobo and I were kids, he threw a stick at a bird and wounded it. I screamed at Bobo. Blue cracks appeared in the sky, followed by a boom like a boulder tumbling down a hillside.

Our mother took me to the valley's shaman, Larry. Shaman Larry made us sacrifice our entire flock of shrews. This seemed to satisfy the sky demon, because we didn't see it for many years.

So, the morning after The Big Orange Ghost Incident, I decided I had to pay Shaman Larry another visit in his cave.

"I have summoned another demon," I told him. "I threw a rock against the wall."

"You have not been careful with your temper," he said.

"I have not," I said, and lowered my head in shame.

He sighed and crossed his legs, adjusting his long white toga. "You will need to sacrifice at least twelve more shrews for your indiscretion."

I told Larry that Brenda and I were stretched a little thin in the shrew department. "But the demon ate thirteen woolly mammoths last night and left."

Larry paused. He cupped his ear. "I'm sorry, it sounded like you said the demon ate thirteen woolly mammoths and left."

"Well, not all of them," I said. "It left some carcasses behind. But I believe it may be satisfied?" I said.

Larry didn't respond.

"Perhaps I just don't throw rocks against walls anymore?" I said. "Perhaps if I just continue leading my life picking berries, it won't return? Perhaps if I just sacrifice the occasional shrew—"

"Show me," Larry said.

He caught me off guard. "Show you what?"

"Show me the woolly carcasses."

***

Shaman Larry was nice enough to let me ride with him on his woolly. When we got back to my place, we saw that Klonch had set up his dining room table in his yard.

"Larry!" Klonch said as he finished setting the table. "You're right on time!"

"This is where The Big Orange Ghost feasted on the woollys," I said. But Larry wasn't listening.

"Klonch, are you eating the demon-infected woollys?" Larry said.

"They're incredible!" Klonch said, stuffing a chunk of meat in his mouth. He tore off another piece and tossed it on a plate. "Have a go!"

Larry approached the plate cautiously.

"These pieces are a little pinker," Klonch said, pointing. "Those pieces are a little darker. We've got the full spectrum."

Larry tore off a piece in the middle and took a bite. He fell back into one of Klonch's dining room chairs. "Oh," he said. He tore off another piece and stuffed it into his mouth.

"Good, right?" Klonch said.

"Incredible," Larry said.

"I don't think The Big Orange Ghost would like us feasting on its kill," I said.

"Oh would you give it a rest, Grog?" Larry said, tearing off another chunk of meat. He looked around Klonch's yard while he munched on it. "Damn, is there any way we could watch a game or something?"

***

Brenda frowned as we mashed berries on our kitchen island. Every once in a while, we would hear the sound of the crowd cheering in Klonch's yard.

"You know," Brenda said. "Klonch is making a fortune selling his woolly mammoth meat."

"I know," I said. I didn't look up from the berries I was mashing.

For a few seconds, the only thing I could hear in our cave was the sound of mushy berries. Then, someone outside must have kicked a neanderthal head into the goal. The crowd went wild.

Brenda sighed and looked up at the ceiling of our cave. "Klonch is also making money selling tickets to his neanderthal head soccer game."

"I know," I said.

"He's so entrepreneurial."

My hand slipped out of the bowl, sending a clump of berry slop onto the ground.

Someone knocked at our door. It was Klonch.

"Hey hey hey," he said, leaning up against my cave wall. "The man of the millennium."

"I'm busy, Klonch," I said.

"Oh, sorry," he said, looking over my shoulder. "I just have a quick favor to ask. The second game is about to start, and we need more meat."

"I don't eat meat."

"Yeah, but you can ask your demon to cast its spells on it. And this second game is set to draw an even larger crowd. Shaman Larry is as hot as The Big Orange Ghost right now."

I looked out at Klonch's yard where Larry dribbled a neanderthal head between some stones. In spite of his long priestly toga, Larry had incredible footwork.

I shook my head. "I'm not summoning a demon so you can sell meat at your soccer match."

"Please, Grog."

"No," I said. And I slowly heaved the cave door closed in his face.

When I turned around, Brenda was putting on her nicest toga.

"What are you doing?" I said.

"I'm going to go watch the game," she said. "See what this magic meat thing is all about."

"You're going to eat an animal?" I screamed.

She rolled her eyes as she walked past the berry mush on the ground. "Enjoy your dinner."

***

I took Bobo's big rock outside and threw it against my cave wall. Who cares if The Big Orange Ghost eats me, I thought. I wasn't meant for this world anyway.

The rock bounced off the wall. A spark landed in some blackened earth.

Nothing.

Interesting, I thought. The Big Orange Ghost was nowhere to be found. Behind me, the crowd cheered as Larry bicycle-kicked a neanderthal head into the goal. His teammates carried him around the field on their shoulders.

I cupped my hands together and pushed a mound of dead leaves and sticks next to the cave wall. The Big Orange Ghost seemed to like feasting on those sorts of things. Perhaps it just needed a snack to entice it to appear.

I threw the rock.

A spark flew.

The snack started smoking.

And The Big Orange Ghost appeared.

"I don't want trouble," I said, holding a stick up to keep it back.

The Big Orange Ghost crackled.

"Don't mess with me," I said.

The Big Orange Ghost started to dim.

"I'm sorry, don't go!" I said, and gave it another stick snack. It grew a little larger. I kept feeding it bigger and bigger sticks until it grew to the size of a baby woolly mammoth. Then, I ran inside and retrieved my stone bowl of berries. I tried holding it over The Big Orange Ghost, but the ghost didn't like that and bit my hand. I set up a contraption with more stones to hold the stone bowl above The Big Orange Ghost, and then I watched as bubbles formed in the berry mush.

Fascinating.

I started fantasizing about what I would do next. I would get my tray, sling it over my shoulder with my spare toga, and fill it up with bowls of hot berry mush. Then, I would go over to the crowd gathered around the soccer match and yell, "Hot berry mush! Get your hot berry mush!"

And Brenda would be so embarrassed. She would look at me with shame. Shame that I was a humble berry seller.

But the crowd would love it. They would say, "Grog, this hot berry mush. It's wonderful."

And I'd go, "Oh, stop."

And they'd say, "No, really. It's truly delightful. How did you make it so hot?"

And I'd wink and say, "Magic."

I'd sell a million. No, two million. And I'd buy a brand new five-bedroom cave and invite Bobo and Katherine over for dinner.

"How did you afford this?" Bobo would ask.

And I'd continue mashing up berries on the counter. "I gave the people what they wanted. And you know what?" I'd say, pausing to lean against the counter. "I didn't have to hurt a single animal to do it."

And he might ask what happened to Bruno, at which point I would quickly change the subject.

"How are you doing that?" A voice said.

***

I had been staring at my bowl of bubbling berry mush for so long, I hadn't realized I had spaced out. I looked up and saw Klonch.

"How am I doing what?" I said.

He pointed at The Big Orange Ghost. He looked hesitant to come any closer. "You've tamed it."

I shrugged. "It's a picky eater. It doesn't like rocks and dirt, so as long as it's surrounded by those things, it doesn't take off running."

Klonch dropped to one knee and bowed his head. "You are a ghost tamer."

More people followed in Klonch's footsteps.

"What is that?" a redheaded woman named Gilgabell said.

"It's a new hot berry mush concoction I've come up with," I said. "It's actually quite simple when you get down to it. You just need a handful of blackberries, a handful of salmon berries, a handful—"

"Grog is a ghost tamer," Klonch said.

Gilgabell dropped to her knee. "Ghost tamer," she said.

A crowd started to form as people wandered from the field to see about the commotion near my cave.

"No offense to the ghost," I said, "but it's just heating the berries. Here, Tony, try a bite."

Tony refused. "Ghost tamer," he said, dropping to his knee.

Word of my ghost taming spread from the front of the crowd to the back. I tried to sell my berry mush, but no one would sample it.

"Sally, try a bowl! Free of charge!"

"I am not worthy, Ghost Tamer."

"Pilvink?"

"I am scum compared to you, Ghost Tamer."

"Mustache Minshew, surely you'll try a bowl of my hot berry mush."

"I will sacrifice myself to your ghost."

I started trying to spoon-feed people. I was sure that if they tried just a smidgen of my delicious berry mush, they would fall in love with it and make me the richest man in the valley. But they all turned their heads, declaring themselves unworthy of my creation. When I demanded that someone indulge in the feast I had prepared, Minshew tried to throw himself on top of The Big Orange Ghost.

As I wrestled him away from my ghost pit, a voice yelled out, "Hey, what's going on here?" It was Shaman Larry. He pushed through the crowd with a neanderthal head in his hands. "What happened to the game?"

"Grog has tamed a ghost," Minshew said. "We are trying to sacrifice ourselves to his greatness."

"To whose greatness?" Larry said. "If anyone is sacrificing themselves, they should sacrifice themselves to me." He poked himself in the chest with his thumb.

Minshew stepped aside so Shaman Larry could get a better look at The Big Orange ghost, who was quite large and loud by this point.

"Damn," Larry said. "It's beautiful."

"This is what Grog used to cook the woollys," Klonch said.

"That was an accident," I said.

"This is no accident," Larry said. He looked at me. "You figured out how to keep it in one place."

I shrugged.

Larry looked around. "Do we, uh, have any woolly mammoths around here?" Everyone shook their heads. "Damn," Larry said. "All right, Minshew, go ahead and heat up one of your arms on it."

"No, wait!" I said. I pointed at one of my bowls of berry mush. "Let's sacrifice some berries to the ghost instead!"

Larry leaned forward a little. "No, that looks pretty gross. We should probably sacrifice some meat. Minshew, your arms, please."

"Wait, wait!" I yelled, panicking. I looked around, trying to think fast. My eyes settled back on Shaman Larry and the neanderthal head in his hands. "Perhaps we can throw the neanderthal head on The Big Orange Ghost," I said.

Larry thought about this for a moment. "I suppose we could eat his brains as an appetizer until we got something more substantive. Klonch, go fetch one of your pet sloths."

"Yes, Shaman," Klonch said, and he took off running for his yard.

Shaman Larry tossed the neanderthal head on the ghost and wiped his hands. "Good thinking," he said, "Ghost Tamer."

As I listened to the sound of the ghost popping and hissing as it ate the neanderthal head, I could see Brenda smiling at me from the crowd.

***

That night, Brenda and I shook our bed like the ground beneath a pack of stampeding wildebeest. Once we'd gotten the bugs loose, we set our bed mat down and made love on it like two hippos reunited after a long sexless drought.

The next day, Shaman Larry came to my cave and invited me up to his house in the hills. We sat on his porch overlooking the valley. He handed me a stone bowl of golden liquid.

"Drink it," he said.

I took a sip. I felt as if a tiny gopher was giving my heart a warm hug. "This is amazing."

"Right?" Larry grinned. "Last night, after your party was over, I sneaked back to your place and fed that demon you summoned in your backyard."

"You did?"

"Yeah. It was hungry. After it came back to life, I threw a bunch of old plants in a stone bowl full of water and heated that sucker up. It made this liquid."

I looked down at the liquid. "What do you call it?"

"I call it beerg. Doesn't it make you just want to kick back in a chair with a chunk of meat and watch a game?"

"I don't eat meat."

"Right, right. Listen, Grog." Shaman Larry turned in his chair and leaned forward earnestly. "I think this demon might be the next big thing. I know you don't eat meat, but you tasted my beerg. It tastes fantastic, no?"

"It does." I took another sip and savored it as it slid across my tongue.

"I'm guessing that your demon can make all kinds of things. We already know it can make existing things taste better. We just need to experiment with it. And then we need to scale it."

I looked around to make sure no one was listening to us. "Should we really be talking about a demon like it's a product?" I whispered. "It just sounds...sacrilegious."

Shaman Larry put his hand on his chest. "Well, I'm not a religious man, but I can see why you might feel that way."

"What do you mean you're not a religious man?" I said. "You're a shaman."

Larry's eyes got really wide for a second. "Damn." He pointed at me. "See, that's what's so great about you, Doug. You get people to let their guards down."

"Grog."

"What?"

"My name is Grog."

"Whatever. Listen. I know some venture capitalists in the valley that would be all over this idea."

"Will they use The Big Orange Ghost to cook meat?"

"Of course. That's the point."

"Then I can't meet with them."

Larry stood up. "Dammit, Grog, what is it with you and meat?"

"I respect every animal's right to live."

"But why, Grog? Why?"

***

I stood up and went to the edge of his porch and leaned against the railing. I looked out at the majestic view of the valley.

"When I was a child," I said, "My brother Bobo and I found a saber tooth tiger cub in a cave. We brought him home and nursed him back to health. We named him Peter." I could feel myself getting choked up. I paused to regain my composure. "We raised Peter to be a full-grown tiger. We used to throw the occasional neanderthal head across the yard and…" I fought back tears. "He would fetch it."

Larry rubbed my back.

My vision blurred with tears as I looked at the beige hills on the horizon. "Then, one day, I came home from picking berries, and Peter was gone. I told my father, and my father said, 'Ah, yes. Bobo threw some rocks at him. Then we ate him.'"

"Your family ate your pet?" Larry said.

I nodded.

Larry patted my shoulder. "I had a similar experience with a parakeet."

"I'm sorry."

"Well, I was the one who ate him, so it's not quite the same story," Larry said. "But go on."

"I ran away from home that day. I vowed to never bring harm to an animal." I looked Larry in the eye. "That goes for any harm my ghosts could cause as well. I'm sorry."

Larry nodded sympathetically. "I understand."

We both looked out at the valley for a moment.

Suddenly, Larry jerked back violently and held his forehead.

"Are you okay?" I said.

"Yeah, totally," he said, still clutching his forehead. His eyes were closed in pain. He jerked back again. "Aiiiiighhhh," he screeched.

"Larry!" I said. "Larry, what's wrong?"

"I'm getting a message from the gods," he said, gritting his teeth. "They're telling me...no, it can't be. They're telling me Peter wants you to start a company. It's fine if you don't want to eat meat. He's cool with that. But he says…don't...don't stop Larry from eating meat."

"He said that?"

"Yes, the message is coming through very clearly." Larry closed his eyes and reached up to the sky with his free hand. "Let Larry heat up food…Wow, now I'm just seeing a flash of images. Garlic. Butter. Rosemary. Fresh shrew stuffed inside a flying squirrel. A plump gazelle smothered in beaver fat. Slow-turned over a Big Orange—"

"Larry," I said.

Larry opened one eye. "Ghost."

"Stop."

"I'm having another vision."

"You're embarrassing yourself."

Larry paused for a moment. Then he started shrieking at the sky, "The gods want us to start the greatest company this world has ever seen—"

"Larry!"

"Okay, fine!" Larry said, dropping his hands to his sides. "But do you not see the potential here?"

"The potential for a vegan company?"

Larry pursed his lips. He pointed at me. "I'll make a deal with you."

"I'm listening."

"I will co-found a vegan company with you," Larry said. "As long as you let me use The Big Orange Ghost to cast its delicious spells on meat for my own consumption."

"You're pushing it, Larry."

"But think of the upside!" Larry said. "If our company converts other people to veganism, what does it matter if I eat meat? Isn't the company still worth it?"

He had a point.

I held up my stone bowl. "Do you have any more beerg?"

***

Claude the venture capitalist set his stone bowl full of beerg down on the granite conference table. "This is life-changing," he said.

"Agreed," said Mindy the venture capitalist.

"How many can you make an hour?" said Theresa the venture capitalist.

"Five," said Larry proudly.

"Five?" Mindy shouted. "There are at least five thousand cavemen and women in this valley. How are we supposed to make a business out of something so scarce?"

"Scarcity is our strength," Larry said.

The venture capitalists looked at each other.

"Is this man the Ghost Tamer?" Theresa said, pointing at me.

I nodded.

"Can you tame a ghost for us right now?" Claude said.

"Larry?" I said.

Larry went outside of the venture capitalists' office cave. He came back dragging a blanket with logs covered in The Big Orange Ghost.

The venture capitalists gasped. They were impressed.

"Make sure not to get too close," I said. "The Ghost will note hesitate to bite you."

Claude's eyes glazed over as he became entranced by The Ghost. "And you are the only mortal who can summon The Ghost?"

I nodded.

"Can we have a moment?" Mindy said.

Larry and I went outside.

"I think they like it," I whispered.

"Are you kidding?" Larry whispered back. "The last guy that came in here pitched a pointier stick. And he got a deal."

"How do you know?"

"How do you think I got the money to buy my cave?"

"Mr. Grog?" Mindy called out from inside the cave.

We walked back inside.

"Mr. Grog, Shaman Larry," Mindy said. "Thank you for bringing in your idea."

"Anytime," Larry said.

"We love it," Claude said.

"But this is not a company," Mindy said.

Larry's jaw dropped.

"It does not scale," Theresa said. "You only have one mortal man who can summon the demon, and even when he does summon it, he's only able to crank out five products an hour."

Larry started to panic. "He can summon a lot of demons. Or perhaps one big demon."

"This is not a business, Larry," Claude said. He tapped the tips of his fingers together. "It's a religion."

Larry paused. "We already have a religion, Claude. The whole valley worships the sun, moon, and stars, and I translate the gods' messages for the valley."

Theresa waved her hands. "That is so terribly old-fashioned."

"We need an upgrade," Mindy said. "Something splashier. Something that says, 'Look right here in front of you. You want to see a god or a demon or whatever? This will burn your face off.'"

"The burning is the appeal," Theresa said. "People need to fear it."

"People need to fear you," Claude said, looking at me.

"I don't want people to fear me," I said.

Mindy nodded. She gestured at me diplomatically. "But you want people to eat their vegetables."

"Yes."

"To do that," Mindy said, "you'll need to threaten to burn them alive."

"But—"

"No buts," Theresa said. "I wouldn't touch a cucumber without the explicit threat of pain and certain death."

I nodded. I thought about my old woolly, Phil. I thought of all the critters roaming around the valley, dodging rocks thrown by Bobo and his gang. I thought of Peter.

"Okay," I said.

"Okay?"

"Okay."

Mindy slapped the table. "Then it's settled," she said. She lifted her stone bowl of beerg. "To Shaman Grog. And his assistant, Larry."

***

"Thank you, Cleveland!" I yelled as the giant straw effigy of a raspberry burned behind me. Larry and I waved to the cheering amphitheater one last time and went behind the curtain. As soon as I was backstage, I collapsed to the ground.

I was exhausted. We had just completed a thirty-valley tour, and the last four valleys were the absolute worst. Pittsburgh, Milwaukee, Little Rock, and a mile to the south, Jacksonville. A year ago, I had never ventured more than ten miles from the cave I was born in. Now, I had been as far as fifty miles away.

The shows were always the same. The village's leaders would force the villagers into the local amphitheater at spear-point. Larry and I would dance around on stage with some flaming sticks. We would instruct everyone in attendance to replace their meat consumption with a strict vegan diet. And then, we would back up our demands by acting out a three-hour play to teach them the lore of The Big Orange Ghost. Sometimes, we would burn a giant straw effigy of a fruit or vegetable as the grand finale. Tonight was one of those nights.

"Here," Larry said, handing me a bowl of beerg.

I snatched it greedily and started chugging. I couldn't remember the last time I had gone more than a few hours without beerg. Maybe the Portland show. I was drinking beerg before, during, and after shows now. It was taking more and more of the stuff to give me that same Tiny Gopher Hugging My Heart feeling.

"Shaman Grog," Minshew said, holding a spear. Minshew tagged along as our bodyguard now. "A Clevelandian has been caught eating meat."

"Well," Larry said, "we just finished giving everyone the instructions to their new religion a minute ago, so I think we're still within the grace period."

"Burn them alive," I said.

Larry looked at me like I was crazy.

"Throw the offender in the raspberry effigy and make the rest of the Clevelandians watch," I said.

Larry reached out to grab my shoulder.

I swatted him away. "Serves him right," I said, slurring my words. The beerg was starting to kick in. I felt the tiny gopher slowly wrap its fluffy arms around my heart.

Minshew nodded solemnly and walked away.

"Come on," I said, clapping Larry on the back. "Let's go to the after party. I heard they have peppers."

***

The party was a who's who of Cleveland's entrepreneurial community. There was the woman who invented the wheel, the guy who invented the stone bowl, and the kooky team of brothers who invented the fedora. Tonight, they were wearing matching zebra togas and their signature hats. They handed me a stick with peppers, onions, and tomatoes.

"It's called a kebab," Jim Fedora told me. "I think it would go great with a spell cast by The Big Orange Ghost.

"Would you mind summoning your demon inside our straw effigy of a pomegranate?" Stan Fedora said.

"As long as you de-summon the demon with some water tomorrow morning," I said.

"Of course, of course," Wayne Fedora said.

I waved my assistants over to drag in some Big Orange Ghost leftover from the show. Everyone cheered as my assistants tossed the ghost logs onto the effigy.

Everyone except a beautiful woman in a leopard toga across the room. She stared at me curiously.

***

"My name's Pazoonga," she said.

"Grog," I said, casually stirring the ice cubes in my beerg. An hour had passed since I'd arrived. Pazoonga and I were at the edge of the patio now, watching the rest of the party dance my meticulously choreographed religious dances around The Big Orange Ghost. I kept an eye out for mistakes.

"What do you do for a living, Grog?" Pazoonga said.

I sighed like everyone asked me this question and I was tired of answering it. "I'm a shaman."

She looked impressed. "Wow, that's cool. I've heard religion is like a really hot space right now."

I shrugged. "You could say that."

"Which religion do you work for?"

I gestured vaguely at the people dancing around The Big Orange Ghost. "Just this one sweeping the nation."

She stared at me, shocked. I was used to this look.

"My cofounder and I started it a year ago," I said. "I thought it would just be a side gig, but we did a couple million in revenue this afternoon."

"A couple million?"

I nodded as I took a casual sip of beerg. "We point spears at people and demand money under the threat of burning them alive."

"That's an interesting business model."

"It's Growth Hacking 101." I took another sip of beerg and paused. "Hey, shouldn't you know all of this already? We just gave a sales pitch to the whole village."

She smiled at me. "I'm just in town for a conference."

Now I was impressed. The only people at this party who hadn't been ushered into the amphitheater at spearpoint today were the elite of the elite of Cleveland. Royals, actors, singers, and of course…

"I'm an entrepreneur," Pazoonga said.

I smiled at her slyly as I stirred my drink. "What's your product?"

"Those ice cubes in your beerg."

I tried to take another casual sip of beerg, but I'm sure it looked more like an impressed sip. "That's cool I guess," I said.

"I also started this Killing As a Service company," she said. "Crocodiles, birds, gross bugs in your house, the occasional human. Sometimes we even kill saber tooth tiger cubs."

The gopher hugging my heart was no longer a gopher; it was The Big Orange Ghost, burning in my chest with the passion of all the stars in the sky above me. But for some reason, it wasn't an angry ghost. Maybe it was the beerg, maybe it was the crowd of people dancing my dance in front of me, or maybe it was simply the head rush of a year of being the hottest shaman on the planet, but the ghost inside my rib cage did not seem mad at all.

"My ex-boyfriend and I founded the company together," Pazoonga said softly. "But we had to break up because he didn't like killing animals." She leaned forward, her eyes on my lips as she inched closer to me. "Do you like killing animals, Grog?"

A pigeon flew into the side of my head. I doubled over, clutching my ear and screaming.

The pigeon dropped a note on the ground next to me. Then, it pooped on my head and left.

"Are you okay?" Pazoonga said, holding my shoulder.

I grunted as I picked up the note. It was from Brenda.

Grog, why haven't you written me?

I crumpled up the note and threw it into The Big Orange Ghost.

"Grog?" Pazoonga said. "Grog, is everything all right?"

I watched the note turn into ghost food.

"Now it is," I said.

***

Pazoonga and I drank beerg and danced around The Big Orange Ghost for hours.

At a certain point, I felt the need to impress her, so I pushed Mustache Minshew into The Big Orange Ghost and danced as he thanked me for sacrificing him.

The inventor of tequila came out and poured everybody shots. The rest of the night was a blur.

We sang my religious songs.

We danced my religious dances.

We ziplined off the roof into the pool.

The last thing I remember was going into the cave mansion's master bedroom with Pazoonga and standing next to a bed.

"Summon your demon for me," she whispered in my ear.

I drunkenly threw my rock at the cave wall until I summoned The Big Orange Ghost in a small pile of sticks.

Pazoonga slipped her toga strap over her shoulder and let the garment fall to the floor. "So tell me, Mr. Inventor Man," she said, her face radiant in the demon's soft glow. "Who's hotter: me or The Big Orange Ghost?"

***

Detroit. St. Louis. Houston. Every city was the same to me now.

I started to wonder if I was just going through the motions. Larry and I would still dance on stage every night, but when we'd get to the part where we'd lock arms and spin around in a circle while the ghost ate a giant turnip behind us, I would think, Is this it? Is this all there is? Even the screams of an animal hunter burning to death started to sound less like punk rock, and a little more like my parents' music. There was also the issue of the beerg, and what it did to my memory.

Had I thrown a spear through a meat-eater in Dallas? Or was that Phoenix? Had I drop-kicked Brenda's pigeon onto The Big Orange Ghost in Memphis? Or Philly? And where the hell had Mustache Minshew gone?

Then, in Reno, I did something bad.

"Just one bite," Larry said to me, egging me on at the after-party. We were alone in the Chief of Reno's cave mansion.

"It's about the principle, Larry," I said.

"But it's delicious," he said. He took another chunk of woolly and stuck it out in front of me. The smell of hot meat wafted up my nostrils like little hands reeling me in by my nose. My mouth watered. Larry had tried to pull this stunt before, but never when I was this beerged-out. My will was weak.

I opened my mouth, but then I snapped it shut and pushed the chunk of meat away. "I can't," I said, covering my eyes. "It makes me think of Phil."

Larry laughed. "It's ostrich meat."

I turned to look. "Ostrich?" I said, peeking through my fingers. "Like the bird?"

"Correct," he said, and took another bite.

I cautiously grabbed the chunk of ostrich and sniffed it. Out of all members of the animal kingdom, birds meant less to me than bugs. At least bugs didn't constantly pester me with letters.

I took a bite. Blood rushed through my body, tingling my extremities.

"What in tarnation?" I said.

Larry grinned. "Right?"

I bit off more of the ostrich. "This is what meat tastes like when it's heated up?"

Larry nodded.

I started devouring the enormous pile of meat on the Chief of Reno's dining room table.

"Muahaha! Muahaha!" Larry cackled. But I didn't care.

I was free.

When I had eaten at least half of the ostrich, and thoroughly stretched my stomach to its limit, I sat back and rested my hand on my belly.

Larry smiled at me. "Did you notice anything odd about that ostrich?"

"I have nothing to compare it to," I said. "I've never eaten ostrich before."

"And you still haven't," Larry said as he pulled a chunk of meat out from underneath the table. He set it down in front of me and turned it around so I could see that this particular chunk still had fur on it. Saber tooth tiger fur.

"Gotcha," Larry said.

I lunged at him with my demon-summoning rock. He laughed as he ducked underneath my clumsy swings.

"Muahaha! Muahaha!"

The door behind us swung open. Larry and I paused to take a look.

"Klonch?" I said.

"Grog!" Klonch shouted, holding the door. His toga was shredded. Sweat poured down bloody gashes on his face. "Something terrible has happened!"

"Klonch, what's going on?" I said.

"It's Pazoonga," he said. "She's started her own religion, and she's conquering Omaha!"

"Omaha?" I said. I hadn't been home in over a year. I thought of Brenda. "Klonch, everyone worships The Big Orange Ghost in Omaha. No one is going to follow her."

"She has the ghost!" Klonch screamed.

"But I'm the only one who knows how to summon the ghost," I said. Then I remembered the time I summoned it in front of Pazoonga. "Oh," I said.

"She has a whole freaking army," Klonch groaned as he collapsed to the ground.

I caught him and held his head in my hands. "Where's Brenda?" I said. I shook the old man until he opened his eyes. "Klonch! Where's Brenda?"

"She's dead, Grog," Klonch whispered. "There was a drought. The only food left was roots. You can't eat those raw. There was plenty of meat around of course, but we couldn't eat it on account of your religious beliefs. So she waited for you...we all waited for you to bring back The Big Orange Ghost to cook our roots, Grog...but you never came home. When Pazoonga came, we were too weak to fight back."

Klonch closed his eyes again. I started shaking him. "Klonch. Klonch!"

Klonch fell back in my arms, his tongue draped across his cheek.

I dropped him to the ground and sprinted out the door.

"Grog, wait!" Larry yelled behind me, but I didn't stop.

I hopped onto Phil II, my most luxurious woolly stallion, and kicked my heels until he started galloping toward the sunset. If my calculations were correct, it would take me at least fifteen minutes to get from Reno to Omaha.

When I was a mile from home, the outline of an army began to appear on the horizon. Larry galloped up next to me on his woolly, Frederique.

"Grog!" Larry said. "Grog! I talked to Klonch. It's hopeless, man."

"Go away."

"Pazoonga's already murdered all the vegans. The only people who survived are your brother and his band of hunters!"

I tightened my grip on the reins. "Then I'm definitely not giving up."

"You have to, man! It's a suicide mission!"

I closed my eyes and concentrated on the sound of Phil II's brilliantly pedicured hooves clopping against the ground. The wind cooled my skin. "Larry, I am thirty beergs deep," I said. "I have accepted my fate."

Larry's face looked gaunt with pain. The past year of red meat and beerg had taken its toll on him, roughening his skin like a neanderthal's. "Is this about the saber tooth tiger meat thing?" he said.

Honestly, I had forgotten about it. "I hate you, Larry."

"I'm sorry!" he said. "I've just been so depressed lately. I thought a prank might do our souls some good."

"I will never forgive you, Larry."

"I know," he said. "But when you die in a few minutes, you can die with the comfort of knowing you didn't die alone." He reached back into his satchel and pulled out my demon-summoning rock, the same rock Bobo had given me so long ago. "Klonch said the drought's been bad."

I couldn't help but smile as I took the rock. A few minutes later, we made a pit stop by my old cave wall to summon an old friend. And a few minutes after that, Larry and I did die. But I wasn't comforted by the fact I didn't die alone. I was comforted by the look in Bobo's and Pazoonga's eyes when they saw two shamen barrelling towards them at high speed on flaming woollys.

***

The next two million years weren't too eventful. I floated above my corpse with Larry for a couple hundred thousand years just reliving our last moments. Time goes a little faster when you're dead, but if you had seen how epic a burning battlefield looks, you'd probably stick around to chat about it too.

We spent another million years or so flying around haunting people's dreams, but then we got bored and returned to our bodies.

I'm not gonna lie. It was super hard to find our bodies after being gone for so long. And the ice age did things to our skin that beerg never did. But we felt attached to our old shells, and decided to keep them company for a while.

Then the archaeologists came. They found my body, but they didn't find Larry's.

"Twenty yards to your left!" I screamed at the archaeologists as they carried my body away. "He's twenty yards to your left!" But they didn't hear me.

"Go," Larry told me.

"I can't just leave you here," I said.

"Shh," he said, and he pressed his finger to my lips. "It's time to move on," he said. And he handed me a fedora.

"Where did you get this?"

"I stole it from Jim's ghost," he said.

For the first time in my entire death, I realized that that was exactly what I was. A ghost. Not big and orange. Just small and transparent.

"By the way," I said. "I wanted you to know that I forgive you, Larry."

"I know," he said. He pointed at the archaeologists as they walked away. "Go."

I followed them to a place called Cleveland. But it wasn't the same Cleveland I knew. This Cleveland was big, intimidating, and far away. It was also the most beautiful thing I had ever seen in my life.

They put me in a glass case in a museum. I floated behind the case for seventy years, lost in my own thoughts as people came and went. Kids, teenagers, moms, dads, and grandparents—all ogling at my warped, twisted face, frozen in time for generations of Clevelandians to stare at. I never stared back.

Until you walked in.

You were wearing a fedora too. And when you led your class of kindergarteners into the museum, you looked as bored and sad as me.

"What happened to him?" a little boy said, pointing at me.

A little girl tugged on your sleeve. "Who was he?"

The rest of your class chimed in as they gathered around my body.

"Did he die in a war?"

"Why is he melting?"

"Is that a spear sticking out of his head?"

And you leaned forward to get a better look at me. "No, kids," you said. "He was just a regular guy."

And then you left.

THE AD GUYS

After years of trying to get a record deal, the alternative rock band The Ad Guys decided to start doing jingles for local businesses. Boba shops. Fertilizer brands. A company that sold surveillance cameras for convenience stores.

Whoooo is that shoplifter
Who who
Who who

In their commercials, all five of The Ad Guys wore kangols and wayfarers and played their instruments. Antoine played bass. Dingxiang played drums. Javier played guitar. And Wally sang.

It was supposed to be a temporary thing. They'd work on their commercials during the day and then play gigs at night. But after a year, their ad business was thriving, while their band could still only book small shows in local bars and coffee shops.

One day, Elon Musk knocked on their door.

"I like your stuff," Elon said, his hands in his pockets, his head bobbing like a turtle testing the air outside of its shell. "I'd like to book you for a commercial."

"Wow!" Antoine said. "For SpaceX?"

"Or Tesla?" Dingxiang said.

"Or Neuralink?" Javier said.

"We don't really do commercials anymore," Wally said. "We're just focusing on our art."

The rest of The Ad Guys glared at Wally. Wally could be such a buzzkill sometimes.

"It's a commercial for SpaceX," Elon said. "A thirty-second spot for the Super Bowl. I don't usually advertise, but your songs are super cool. I need it in a week. I'll give you a million dollars. So, good luck." And then he walked off.

The Ad Guys stared at Wally.

"Fine," Wally said. "One more commercial."

The Ad Guys spent the next twenty-four hours in the studio, coming up with new jingles.

I'm getting hot as an oven
For some Red Planet Lovin'

No.

I've been dreaming
Of a terraformed
Atmosphere

No.

We don't
We don't
We don't blow up anymorrrrre

No.

Hop on a rocket and lose your feces
'Cause homo sapiens are going to be the first multi-planetary specieeeeeees

Around 11 am, Javier started having a panic attack. He sucked on his inhaler while he rested his chin on the neck of his Maestro Vibrola.

"We're not going to make it," Javier said.

"Nope," Antoine said.

"Stop it," Dingxiang said. "We have six days to film the commercial, and we already have the jingle."

"What jingle?" Antoine said.

Dingxiang started up the beat to Red Planet Lovin'. "Let's just go with this one."

"I can't believe we're going to lose the SpaceX account," Javier said.

"Can't believe, can't believe," Antoine sang as he plucked a somber bass line.

"Twenty-One Pilots is going to take it from us." Javier said, taking another hit of his inhaler. "I swear."

"Would you shut up?" Dingxiang said.

Antoine laid down something funky. "It doesn't really matter that everything's on fire, 'cause Elon wants to start an inter-galactic empirrrrre."

Dingxiang started playing Red Planet Lovin' again.

Javier rocked back and forth in his chair, crying as his bandmates battled each other with their melodies.

"I'm getting hot as an oven—"

"Intergalactic empirrrre—"

"Quiet," said a voice across the room. Everyone stopped to turn and look. It was the lead singer, Wally. He was supine on the couch, swaddled in his tie-dye trench coat. He took off his John Lennon glasses. "We need something irreverent."

"Red Planet Lovin' is full of communist sexual innuendo," Dingxiang said.

"But it's too tame." Wally stood up. "And it's too catchy."

"Elon said he likes our other songs. Our other songs are catchy."

"I don't give a damn what Elon thinks."

The band fell silent.

Wally sighed. "Have you guys forgotten why we started this ad agency in the first place?" Wally gestured around their studio. The instruments. The amps. The mics. The framed posters of Khruangbin and Radiohead. "All we wanted to do was make enough money for our band to tour. And if you haven't noticed, we've got more than enough in savings. That payday loan jingle alone could pay for a three-city tour!"

The band nodded. They knew the jingle.

It's raining money!
Hallelujah!
It's raining money!

Wally slapped one of Dingxiang's cymbals. "So let's flip Elon Musk the bird, ditch this corporate bullshit, and pack the van for Bakersfield!" Wally raised his arms high above his head.

His bandmates looked at each other.

"I think…"

"Ummm…"

"Couldn't we make a lot of money from this ad campaign?" Javier said.

"Like a million dollars," said Antoine.

Wally hung his head.

"If we do the campaign for Elon," Antoine said, "we could do a longer tour."

"And we wouldn't have to go to Bakersfield," Dingxiang said.

"Wouldn't have to go to Bakersfieeeeld," Antoine sang, plucking his bass.

"Fine," Wally said. His bandmates looked up cautiously. "But if we're doing the campaign for Elon, we're doing it my way."

***

Wally opened his laptop with trembling hands. "Just a moment," he said, tapping keys.

Elon Musk sat in the back of the conference room, his legs crossed, his face frozen in its usual pensive expression.

"Everything all right, Wally?" Elon said. "I'm, like, really super psyched for your commercial."

"Everything's fine," Wally said. He turned off the lights and looked back at his bandmates. They stood on either side of a big projector screen, fiddling with their instruments. Wally gave them the thumbs up. "Whenever you're ready."

"I'm ready," Elon said.

"All right," Wally said, his voice shaking. "Hit it, boys," he said, and hit the enter key on his laptop. A video started playing on the projector screen while Antoine played a slow, hypnotic groove on his bass. Dingxiang and Javier followed his lead.

Onscreen, a baby chick hatched out of an egg. A salmon lept upstream. A giraffe gave birth.

Wally started singing in an ominous baritone.

Earth...
Is our home

Shooting stars streaked across the night sky. A dolphin jumped out of the water and did a backflip. An avalanche smothered a mountainside.

The only…
Home we've known

Villagers from a remote tribe fished in a river. New Yorkers crossed a busy street.

But space…
Holds endless wonder

A satellite floated above the Earth. Winds tossed sand around the surface of mars. The Millennium Falcon flew over a planet.

And it kind of makes me wonder…

The band fell silent.

Why are we still on Earth?

Onscreen, an image of Mars split into a kaleidoscope of spinning red planets. The band kicked back into high gear as Wally pulled the microphone out of the stand and sang at the ceiling.

Fuck Earth!
Fuck Earth!
We don't need this planet anywayyyyyyyyy

Fuck Earth!
Fuck Earth!
Blasting off to the motherfucking stars, man

Wally, Javier, and Antoine leaned into the same microphone to sing the bridge.

It doesn't matter if we pollute
Burn down the forests
And melt the glaciers

Kill all the coral
And cut down the tree-eees
Human beings are the only cool specieeeeeeeeeeeeeeeeeeeeeeeeees

Dingxiang pounded his drums.

So Fuck Earth!
Fuck Earth!
We don't need this planet anywayyyyyyyyy

Fuck Earth!
Fuck Earth!
Jump on a rocket and start from scratch, man

Fuck Earth!
Fuck Earth!
Planet Earth is so 20th century

Fuck Earth!
Fuck Earth!

Earth is a Boomer and Mars is Gen-Z

Javier hopped up on the conference table and tore apart a wicked guitar solo. When he hit the final note, the commercial ended with a SpaceX rocket exploding above earth's atmosphere.

Wally turned the lights on.

"It's just the first draft—" Wally said.

"I love it," Elon said.

"Really?" Wally said.

"I can't believe we didn't think of this before," Elon said, slapping his palm against his forehead. "Fuck Earth. We're going to Mars, bitches."

The Ad Guys looked around at each other, grinning.

"Boys, why don't you have a seat?" Elon said. "I have my own presentation to give you."

***

"Gentlemen," Elon said, standing beside an image of himself on the projector screen, "do any of you know the name of my first company?"

The Ad Guys, seated around the conference table, looked at each other.

"Zip2?" Antoine said.

"No."

"X.com?" Javier said.

"No."

"Paypal?" Dingxiang said.

"No, no, no, no, no," Elon said. He clicked to the next slide: an image from the early 90s of five men with dyed hair giving bedroom eyes to the camera. "The Backstreet Boys were my first company."

Wally raised an eyebrow. "Lou Pearlman started the Backstreet Boys."

"No," Elon said, clicking to a slide with a picture of himself with his arms around the Backstreet Boys, "he didn't." Elon clicked to a picture of Silicon Valley. "I secured series A funding for the Backstreet Boys in 1994. I launched them as a prototype in Germany in 1995 and then officially launched them as a product in Sweden later that same year. I made my first million off of their hit single We've Got it Goin' On, which I wrote.

Antoine took out his phone and looked up the song We've Got it Goin On. Sure enough, Elon Musk was the sole songwriting credit. "My god."

"You made your first million off of...a boy band?" Javier said.

Elon nodded "After The Backstreet Boys IPO'd on the Shanghai Stock Exchange, I decided to replicate their success by starting a new company." Elon clicked to the next slide. "N'SYNC."

The Ad Guys all looked back and forth between Elon Musk and the picture of the frosted-tip fivesome on the projector screen.

"No," Wally said.

"You better believe it," Elon said. "And that's not all." Elon continued clicking his clicker. "The Lyte Funky Ones. 98 Degrees. The Jonas Brothers. One Direction. BTS. They're all Elon Musk companies. They are my sole source of income."

"What about Tesla, Solar City, Neuralink, SpaceX—" Antoine said.

"Don't care," Elon said. "They're all fronts for me to chase my true passion: creating beautiful, androgynous, infinitely catchy startups."

The Ad Guys rubbed their foreheads.

"I know this is a lot to take in," Elon said. "But I think you know what comes next."

Dingxiang looked up. "You want us to—"

"You'll need to lose the instruments," Elon said. "They're hideous. And we need to see how you'll look with these tiny nude-colored headsets." Elon tossed them their pop star headsets. They tried them on. "Beautiful," Elon said. "I think you have a lot of potential."

"So this was all a trick?" Wally said. "There was no commercial? You were just scouting your next boy band?"

"Oh, there's a commercial, all right," Elon said, clicking to a slide with Nick Jonas holding a Pepsi. "You see, all boy bands are secretly ad agencies. I didn't just pick the boys for their good looks, swooning voices, and popping dance moves. I hand-picked them for their marketing skills." Elon clicked to a picture of The Ad Guys he'd taken off their website. The picture was taken a year earlier, when they all had peach fuzz on their faces, and they were barely making $100 a week from ads about jarred pickles. "I think your song Fuck Earth has the potential to not only be an international advertisement sensation," Elon said, "but also a top-ten hit on the Billboard Hot 100." He stretched his arms out wide. "So, what do you say, boys? Do you want to become the world's next pop heartthrobs?"

The Ad Guys looked at each other. Except for Wally. He scooted his chair back and stood up. "All right, thanks, Elon," Wally said, tucking in his chair. "But we're real musicians making real music." He gestured for Elon to leave.

"I thought you were an advertising agency," Elon said.

Wally paused. "That's just our day job. Our real passion is making serious artistic music. So, sorry, but being a boy band doesn't really fit into our artistic vision. Right, guys?"

The Ad Guys stared back at him.

"I mean," Javier said, "it could fit into our vision."

"Please excuse my friend Javier," Wally said to Elon. "We have a tour in Bakersfield—"

"Couldn't we just do the pop star thing for just a little bit?" Dingxiang said. "You know, keep making money, save up, and then become serious musicians?"

Wally sighed. "Fine," he said.

"All right!" the rest of The Ad Guys said, jumping up in the air in unison.

***

Alas, The Ad Guys found it a little more difficult to do the pop star thing for "just a little bit." Forty-five minutes after Fuck Earth was released, Spotify's servers crashed from too many users streaming the song.

The success of their first single meant an album was quick to follow. Then a world tour. Then The Ad Guys reached a pinnacle of success never touched by Elvis, The Beatles, or Michael Jackson: all fourteen tracks on their debut album reached the top 14 on the Billboard Hot 100:

1. SpaceX: Fuck Earth
2. Nike: Just don't think about the sweatshops
3. Google: Be evil
4. Exxon: Hot planet summer
5. Facebook: What do you have to hide?
6. Juul: So easy to smoke, a kid could do it
7. McDonald's: Healthy at every size
8. Coca-Cola: Diabetecize your life
9. Smith and Wesson: Arming teachers since 1852
10. Big Pharma: The original opiate for the masses
11. Dupont: Poison is the spice of life
12. Uber: Actually, drivers aren't people too
13. Wal-Mart: Everyday low wages
14. Amazon: Put mom and pop shops in a retirement home

As Jimmy Fallon put it, The Ad Guys' level of celebrity was like Kim Kardashian and Donald Trump had a baby with Michael Jordan. At least, that's what he said when he introduced The Ad Guys on The Tonight Show after they wrapped up their world tour.

"The Ad Guys, everybody!" Jimmy Fallon said, raising his hands in the air. The audience went wild. Some of the fan girls in the studio audience wore fake mustaches to look like Dingxiang. Others wore Antoine's signature kilt or Javier's space helmet. But more than 80% of the crowd was buttoned up in one of Wally's tie-dye trench coats co-branded with Gucci.

"Welcome back, guys, haha," Jimmy Fallon said.

"Good to be here," Javier said.

"Haha, so, you all look great," Jimmy Fallon said. "Are you all wearing your own fashion label's stuff?"

"Actually, it's wearable art," Wally said. "We don't have our own fashion lines just for the sake of making money."

"No, of course not," Jimmy Fallon said. "I'm so sorry. I just meant you look great."

"Our looks are really secondary to our music," Wally said. "We're mostly just focusing on our music right now."

"Definitely," Jimmy Fallon said. "And let's talk about your music." Jimmy Fallon pulled out a vinyl copy of Fuck Earth and showed it off for the cameras. The cover art was a painting of a giant hand pressing a cigarette into the earth. "I'm going to go ahead and ask the question everyone is dying to ask you guys," Jimmy Fallon said. "What's the next company you're going to write a song about?"

Wally glared at Jimmy Fallon.

***

"Wow guys, that was so super great, right?" Elon Musk said as he and The Ad Guys rode back from The Tonight Show in a limousine.

The Ad Guys all looked at Wally, who stared out the window.

"What?" Elon Musk said. "Did you guys not have a good time?"

"We had a great time," Antoine said, adjusting his kilt as he crossed his legs. "Wally—not so much."

"What are you talking about?" Wally said sarcastically. "I loved every minute."

Dingxiang rolled his eyes. "Oh come on. During the Wheel of Musical Impressions segment, you were supposed to sing The Star Spangled Banner like a Nickelback song, but you just ranted about capitalism for five minutes."

"And?" Wally said. "They asked me to sing the capitalist theme song in the tone of corporate fascist pop muzak." He crossed his arms. "My rant had the same sentiment."

"And what was your sentiment during Lip Sync Battle when you held up signs that said you were being held hostage by a Big Tech oligarch?"

Wally shrugged. "It just felt right."

"Did it just feel right during Box of Lies when you told Jimmy Fallon there was a quartet of pop music sell-outs in box number four?"

"For the record," Wally said, "he thought I was telling the truth."

"I think you were telling the truth!" Javier said. "The truth about how you feel about this band!"

"Psh. Band," Wally said. "Is that what we are? Singing about Uber and McDonald's?"

"You wrote all our songs!" Antoine said.

"I wrote them ironically!" Wally said, slapping his knee.

The limo fell silent.

"Hasn't anyone noticed that yet?" Wally yelled. "Everyday Low Wages?? Put Mom and Pop Shops in a Retirement Home?? Fuck Earth?? What am I? A psychopath? I was trying to destroy these companies!"

The Ad Guys looked at each other.

"All of our clients saw increased profits after our campaigns," Dingxiang said.

"I know!" Wally screamed. "What is wrong with the world!"

Antoine shook his head slowly. "You know, Wally. Maybe the problem isn't the world. Maybe the problem is you."

Wally looked around at his bandmates. Dingxiang squinted out the window. Javier scrutinized his signature Javier Kix shoes. "Is that how you all feel?" Wally said.

"Your songwriting is great, Wally," Dingxiang said. "But offstage, you can be a bit of a downer."

"Offstage?" Javier said. "He's told multiple arenas full of fans that he's a prisoner in a proto-fascist capitalist dictatorship."

"Prove me wrong," Wally said.

"Prove to us that you still want to be in this band," Antoine said.

Wally turned away.

"That's what I thought," Antoine said. "You don't believe in us."

The limousine pulled up to a red light.

"Maybe you're right," Wally said. "Maybe I should go solo." He threw open the door and dashed off into the night.

***

Wally wandered the streets of New York, hoping that maybe, somehow, no one would recognize him. In Times Square, one of The Ad Guys' Coca-Cola commercials played on the Megatron. In the commercial, The Ad Guys performed a flash mob style dance in the hallways of a hospital with nurses and doctors. Each of the band members were hooked up to two IVs: one for insulin, and the other feeding them soda intravenously through their brachial arteries. The IV tubes flailed around in the air as they danced in their hospital gowns.

"Hey, is that Wally?" said one Bulgarian tourist to another.

Wally pulled up the lapels of his tie-dye trench coat and hid his face.

"It is!"

Wally took off running. He didn't stop until he reached Tom's, an underground dive bar with live music. Wally sat in the back, behind the crowd and as far away from the stage as possible.

"No way," a waitress said as she approached his table. Wally slipped her a few hundreds and pressed his finger to his lips. The waitress nodded. "If you want the stage, it's yours," she said as she tucked the bills into her apron. She gestured up at the bar's small stage, where an open-mic guy with a man bun played a Vance Joy song on an acoustic guitar.

"I'm not going to play anything from Fuck Earth," Wally said.

The waitress shrugged. "Play whatever you want."

Wally slipped her a few more hundreds and pointed at the guy onstage. "Ask him if I can borrow his guitar."

***

"What's up, New York?" Wally said.

The crowd in Tom's went wild.

"You might have heard of my band." Wally's fingers trembled as he tuned his guitar. He wasn't sure why he was so nervous. There weren't more than a hundred people in the crowd. Just two days prior, The Ad Guys had performed in front of 70,000 people in Berlin. "I hope you don't mind if I try out some new material on you guys."

The crowd cheered. A half-dozen girls had trouble controlling their screaming.

Wally started plucking a few notes.

"This song is called Naomi," Wally said.

He started singing.

Naomi…
Sometimes it feels as if you don't even
Know me…

The first sign that something was wrong was that all the screaming girls fell silent. Wally noticed that the people in the front row all looked perplexed.

Wally wrapped up Naomi to a few scattered claps.

"This next song is called Bluebirds Take Flight," Wally said.

I see them dancing in the air—

"Play Fuck Earth!" someone in the audience screamed.

Wally kept playing Bluebirds.

"Play the Juul song!" another person screamed.

"Play the Exxon Mobil song!"

By the time Wally finished Bluebirds, he was soaked in sweat. "All right, I hope you all liked that."

The crowd started booing.

"This next song is called Effervescent Charm," Wally said. He started singing.

The crowd really started to turn on him now. They hated Effervescent Charm. They threw gluten-free cheddar popcorn at him. They splashed his feet with craft beer. They demanded he play the Wal-Mart song. They balled their fists and cursed him, and then they took out their iPhones and filmed themselves cursing him.

Wally thought fast. He switched up the guitar riff and started singing.

You say you want a revolution…
Well you know…
It's going to be a lot harder to run a capitalist economy after a revolution…

The crowd quieted down. People stopped throwing popcorn at him. But they weren't fully placated.

Wally pivoted into another song.

Hey Jude
...don't be sad
There's a box on your porch for you to open.

When Wally saw a few people put their arms around each other and start swaying to the music, he knew he was safe for the time being. He just had to keep playing songs from The Ad Guys' unreleased Revisionist Beatles album to satiate the crowd's appetite.

We all live in debt slavery (hey!)
Debt slavery (ho!)
Debt slavery
And we sailed across the sea
In a land of debt slavery

Back in the USSR
You don't know how lucky you are
To no longer live in a centrally planned economy

Shake it up baby now
Shake it up baby
Twist off that bottle of Miller Lite

Dr. Pepper in the Sky with Tiffany Diamonds!

Halfway through the album, the hypnosis was complete. The entire audience in Tom's had their eyes closed. They danced around in the slow, trance-like movements of the latest TikTok dance craze: pulling their wallets out of their pockets, unsheathing their credit cards, identifying the CVV code, entering their information into an online form, and clicking the purchase button.

I never told you
I never told you
How much I loved you
...Scarlet

Suddenly, every audience member's eyes snapped wide open. Wally felt his throat start to close in panic. He knew what the crowd was thinking. A ballad? A ballad about a girl? He thought he could slip in one of his personal songs, but the contrast with the corporate pop had been too stark. He tried to switch to the song You Can, In Fact, Buy Me Love...With A Range Rover, but it was too late. The crowd had become hysterical. They threw ice at him. They splashed Patron on his guitar. They broke Corona bottles and threatened him with the glass shards. Then they jumped on the stage.

A troupe of security guards escorted Wally off the stage while they beat back the crowd with nightsticks.

The guards led Wally up to a private interior balcony on the second floor, far away from the raging crowd below.

They sat him down in a booth next to Elon Musk.

***

"Wow," Elon Musk said. "Wally. Your performance. Don't worry about what the crowd thinks. Naomi? I'm crying. Your emotion—"

"How did you find me?" Wally said.

Elon nodded. "I followed the tracking chip in your neck."

Wally sighed and leaned over the railing. The mob was starting to get really violent now. A guard tackled a guy before he could light the stage curtains on fire. "Do you put chips in all of your boy bands?"

Elon grinned. "Just the members I want to keep." He snapped his fingers, and Justin Timberlake came out of the shadows. "JT, have a seat."

Justin Timberlake sat down across from Wally. "Wally!" JT said. "Listen. Huge fan. Huge. Fuck Earth? Chef's kiss, brother. How did you do it? No, wait! Don't even try to tell me. I get it. An artist never gives up his secret sauce."

Elon Musk patted Justin Timberlake on the head. "JT, would you mind getting us some drinks?"

Justin Timberlake stood up and spun in a circle. "I'm on it." He danced over to the bar, shooting at the ceiling with finger guns.

"One of my finest inventions," Elon said. He shook his head. "But he's starting to malfunction."

"What?" Wally said.

"I want you to replace him."

"You want me to replace Justin Timberlake?"

"I want you to be better than Justin Timberlake." Elon Musk sipped a purple liquid from a test tube, then deposited the empty vial in his breast pocket. "The Ad Guys are like a tech startup at the peak of the dot-com bubble. It's time to pivot the company. Time to get lean. Another solo artist is just what the doctor ordered."

"Elon," Wally said. "I'm not making corporate pop songs anymore. Okay? I'm going solo, but I'm going to work on my own projects."

"And how is that working out for you?" Elon Musk said. On the stage below, security guards dragged away rioters kicking and screaming.

"I'm still working on my new material," Wally said.

Elon leaned over the table. "When I finished programming the prototype of Justin Timberlake, I thought it might be a good idea to let his AI write its own debut single. I was cocky. I had just made a huge breakthrough in robotics that allowed him to dance, and I thought his songwriting AI was equally advanced." Elon looked at Justin Timberlake with shame. "Then he gave me Like I Love You." Elon Musk rubbed his forehead. "The day it was released, domestic convenience store profits plummeted."

"Convenience stores?"

"I know, right? The subliminal messaging was too subtle. I tried to save it with the music video, but it was too little too late. How could his machine learning algorithm be so arrogant?"

"I don't understand."

"Neither did I. It took me months to find the solution."

"What?"

Elon reached out and poked Wally in the heart. "He needed the human component. So I stepped in and wrote his next piece of corporate propaganda, Cry Me A River."

"I thought Cry Me A River was about Britney Spears."

Elon looked amused. "Come on, Wally. The lyrics. The beat. The music video. The entire thing was a blatant advertisement for Home Depot."

Wally sat back in his seat in disbelief. He looked over the railing. Some of the rioters had gone to Taco Bell and come back to throw Queso Chicken Chalupas at the security guards.

"What do you need me for?" Wally said. "Why don't you just build another Justin?"

Elon chuckled. Then his face grew serious. "Wally, you're the most popular musician in history."

"A hundred Justin Timberlakes is better than one Wally," Wally said.

Elon shook his head. "I've already made several thousand. But it doesn't matter how many I make. No Justin Timberlake software program could write a song that pretends to hate a company while secretly loving it as much as you do."

"I'm not pretending. I genuinely loathe these companies."

Elon pointed at him. "Uncanny."

"I'm serious, Elon."

Elon Musk threw up his hands. "You're right. You're the genius here. I don't know how you do what you do, but whatever subliminal jedi mind tricks you use to sell products, they work."

"We're done here," Wally said, and he started to stand up. Elon grabbed him by the wrist and yanked him back into his seat. The look in Elon's eyes scared Wally. It was almost as if Elon was staring directly into his soul, examining its essence, and calculating its utility.

"I know you, Wally," Elon said, still holding him by the wrist. "I know you listen to old bootlegs of Grateful Dead concerts while your bandmates talk to groupies on the tour bus. I know you sleep on the floor of your home studio so you can start working on your acoustic album as soon as you wake up. And I know that while the rest of The Ad Guys are at Jake Paul's house smoking hookah and swimming with wild pigs, you're sitting on the edge of a big rock in Catalina writing lyrics in a leatherbound notebook." Elon let go of Wally's wrist. "Just hear me out," Elon said. "Please."

Wally looked over the railing. More rioters had come back from shopping sprees to throw Yeezies, Supreme roller bags, and Kylie Jenner lip balm at the security guards. One rioter used a Brunello Cucinelli turtleneck to choke out a guard.

"Fine," Wally said.

Elon Musk pulled out some large glossy photographs and spread them across the table. The photos were of a landfill, a baby seagull choking on a plastic water bottle, and miles and miles of trash floating in the water. "I had one of the nerds at SpaceX run some numbers," Elon said, straightening the pictures, "if we put out an album where every song is about a plastic product, it's possible we could have more trash than water in the Pacific Ocean by 2025."

Wally stared at the photo of the baby seagull. It had somehow lodged most of a sixteen-ounce bottle of Dasani down its gullet. Only the bottom of the bottle protruded from its gaping beak. Made from 100% Recycled Plastic.

"You want me to put out a plastic album?" Wally said.

Elon laughed. "It's already in post-production. It will be your replacement band's first album."

"Our replacement band?"

"Did you think your little boy band was going to last forever? It's BLINC's time to shine now."

Wally looked back at the photo of the ocean of trash. "Then what do you want me for?"

"I want you to be part of a much larger project."

"What project?"

Elon smirked. "The future of music." He slid a SpaceX business card with Wally's name on it across the table. "How does 'Executive VP of Audio' sound to you?"

Wally picked up the business card. He stared at it for what seemed like an eternity.

"So this is what you meant by going solo," Wally said.

The edge of Elon's mouth curled into a sly smile. A shadow cast across his face as he nodded. "I want you to bring music to the rest of the universe."

"I got mojitos!" Justin Timberlake said, startling them both. JT looked around, his AI sensing distress. "You guys good?"

Wally grabbed one of the mojitos. Elon Musk watched him carefully."To fuck Earth," Wally said as he raised his cup.

Elon smiled and raised his own cup. "To fuck Earth."

Down below, the security guards had subdued the mob, and began dragging out the last of the protestors by their ankles. The exit door slammed, and as Wally, Justin Timberlake, and Elon Musk took the first sip of their mojitos, Tom's became eerily quiet.

In one erratic motion, Wally tossed his drink into Justin Timberlake's face and took off running. Justin Timberlake flailed his arms as sparks jumped from his smoking hardware.

"Stop him!" Elon yelled as Wally ran.

Elon's security guards blocked the stairs, so Wally took a hard right and pushed through the doors to the terrace and jumped off the balcony. Shocks of pain ran up his knees when he landed, but he kept going.

He didn't stop running until he reached Times Square. In the glow of the movie-theater-sized screens that surrounded him, he stumbled forward, doubled-over as dozens of fans snapped pictures of him on their phones. They wanted him to sing Fuck Earth. They wanted him to do the Exxon Mobil TikTok dance. And then the screaming started.

Something hit Wally in the face. The something hit him again, and this time, Wally realized the something was Justin Timberlake's robotic arm; Elon Musk had ripped it off at the shoulder, and was using it to flog Wally in the face.

Elon struck Wally a fourth time with JT's arm, sending Wally to the ground. As Wally lay there, he wondered about all the fans around him using their phones to film the scene. Eventually, they would upload the footage to Twitter, but how would the world interpret what they were seeing? What would the New York Times headline be?

Meme Entrepreneur Uses Pop Legend's Arm to Beat Music Icon to Death?

Or would everyone assume they were witnessing a stunt? A gag? A Tonight Show segment with Jimmy Fallon ready to pop out at any moment?

Or, Wally thought, to his horror: would they think this was all an ad?

The Time Square Megatron screen started blasting a commercial for Dr. Pepper. A Dr. Pepper can cracked open against a bright red background. Cola gushed in the air like a soda geyser.

In sync with the ad, Elon hit Wally again, sending a blood spatter into the crowd.

The crowd cheered.

***

Wally woke up in a cryogenic pod. He pushed the glass door above him and stepped out. He looked around. He was in a small room with a kitchenette, a toilet, a fridge, and a small flatscreen television next to his sleeping pod. He turned on the television. Some smooth jazz played against a black background. Elon Musk's face came into view.

"Oh, hey," Elon Musk said. "Wow. So cool. Good morning. And welcome to Mars. I have some bad news for you. You have been asleep for a hundred years, and all of your friends, family, and bandmates are dead. The good news is: all of your enemies are dead as well. Except for me, although I hope you consider me a friend. So you have one friend left, me, and I'll be joining you in about six months when my ship lands. So, enjoy Mars and, um, start thinking of the planet's theme song."

The TV flickered off, and one of the tiles on the floor slid away. A little elevator brought up an acoustic guitar in a stand.

Wally went to the window and pulled the blinds. Outside was a Hard Rock Cafe next to a Whataburger. In the background, he could see more buildings—a Cheesecake Factory, a Shell gas station, an AMC movie theater, and more. Beyond those: the barren desert landscape of Mars.

Wally grabbed the guitar and sat cross-legged on his sleeping pod. He strummed a few chords and looked at the red hills in the distance for inspiration. If he squinted, he could almost block out the neon glow of the signs outside his window.

THE TOMATO THIEF

Your grandma is stealing tomatoes again. You know the tomatoes. Those fat, heirloom-shaped ones with a greenish hue around the stem. The ones in those garden boxes hung outside the ground floor windows of her senior center. The ones she's been stashing inside her purse for ages. Those tomatoes. You knew she was filching the plump bastards. You knew the whole time. How else would she have been able to prepare such farm-to-table fresh salads without a car to drive to the grocery store? Sure, she could have asked Phil, the former opiate addict and current caretaker at Sunset Valley Semi-Retirement Community and Squash Club, to pick her up some, but you knew it wasn't a coincidence that the tomatoes were always same-day fresh when you came to visit. Never next-day fresh. Same-week fresh be damned. Those crispy sweet succulents were plucked mere minutes before you strolled through the double doors, and you knew it. But you've never caught her in the act.

Until today. Today, when you drive up to Sunset Valley, you see granny hanging around outside one of the garden boxes on the ground floor. Her back is turned to you, her face in profile as she side-steps in perfect rhythm with your car, careful to always keep herself between you and the crime. The way she glances over her shoulder, she looks like a seasoned bank robber calculating the time for the police sirens to close in.

You park, and as you walk up the drive, your grandma continues her chicken shuffle from one end of the garden box to the other. As you edge closer, you start to see them: hints of red flesh in between her liver-spotted fingers. She's pulling fistfuls of tomatoes out of her purse and hastily tossing them back in the box with the same careless motion of an old man feeding crumbs to a duck. The nerve of this woman.

You're close enough to confront her now, but she's finished the hack-job of a cover up. Now she's innocently brushing aside the leaves of the vine, a disingenuous look of astonishment stretching the corners of her face. Without even the dignity of a greeting, the sociopath invites you to look at the strange phenomenon she's stumbled upon, a baffling paranormal event in the same supernatural realm as crop circles. You see what she's pointing at: three dozen red orbs sitting in the topsoil. Tomatoes off the vine.

"Ah, yes, well, how did that happen?" you ask, but the cold-blooded criminal didn't really want your opinion anyway. She already has suspects in mind. She has a batch of half-baked conspiracy theories. She wants to discuss motive. She takes your hand and leads you in a slow march back to the castle.

When you finally reach the front door, you interrupt her diatribe to ask her what her next activity is. Exercise class, she says. She just got done with choir, now it's time for exercise, and this afternoon she'll play Bridge with Doris. Then Bingo. Then karaoke. Then Mahjong before she rounds out the evening with virtual bowling and a pasta making class. You had forgotten your grandma lives in what is essentially a cruise ship.

She opens the door. The heat is palpable. As soon as you set foot in this greenhouse, you are enveloped in the humid hug of a lobby with every thermostat cranked to plastic-melting temperatures. You think about requesting a dial-down of said thermostats, but you know you will be the one outlier in an otherwise unanimous preference for a climate hovering somewhere around 'deep jungle.'

Your grandma takes you to the exercise room, which is also the board game room and movie room and Republican Women's Luncheon room. There is a very large portrait of Ronald Reagan hung near an abandoned game of Clue. There are also people. Lots of people. Sitting (all of them), above eighty (most of them), and old enough to not be asked to remove their shoes at airport security (all of them). They yell at each other in hoarse, courteous voices which, in a vacuum, would be loud enough to be understood, but are no match for the forty other voices battling for comprehension. Most of the elders stop yelling as soon as they see your grandma, and all are quiet when your grandma drops you off in the corner, and takes her position at the front of the room. Your momentary confusion is quickly replaced by the amusing revelation that your grandma isn't just attending an exercise class; she's leading one.

And lead she does. A clap of her hands, a quick scolding to a troublemaking septuagenarian in the back, one swift poke to a cassette player on a table, and the exercise begins. Forty-one members of the greatest generation, all scowling, all breathing out of their mouths, all still hunched in rows of tan metal folding chairs, lift their arms above their respective heads, and lean side-to-side to the 1982 post-disco funk classic, Billie Jean. The sight puts pressure on the soul from every angle.

Then Phil enters the room. You know, Phil. Phil Sneed. The recovering opiate addict. The male nurse decked in robin's blue scrubs and white sneakers with four-inch-thick soles. The mustachioed former all-SWAC wrestler at Grambling State and current MVP of a bowling team with a name you can't quite remember but which you're pretty sure is a painfully unsubtle reference to the 300 Spartans or something. You know, Phil. Phil Sneed.

A little rush of self-righteousness circulates through your system when you see him. Your step is full of pep as you stride over to meet him, ready to blow the whistle on the tomato thief, who, in all her wrist flicking glory, is still on her imaginary stage, still pulling the strings of forty-one ancient marionettes creaking, cracking, and cartilage-popping their way through a hideous bastardization of the crowd wave. You're five paces away from Phil—who only came into the room to pick up the deserted game of Clue on the window seat—but five paces is length eternal when you're about to rat out a family member. While the forest of fleshy arms continues to rustle in your peripheries, a dark cloud crosses your mind and begins to rain intrusive thoughts.

You think about the scrunched mix of sadness and disgust on your spouse's face when you admitted to the affair.

Out of the corner of your eye, eighty hands, half a stump, and one hook have started quivering in the air.

You remember the hummingbird fluttering its wings in your tummy when you saw the red and blue lights in your rearview, right before you got the DUI.

Third row from the back, a retired patent attorney tears his labrum. He fights through the pain, using his good hand to hold up his withered wrist.

Somewhere, tucked away in the back of your mind's filing cabinet is the number to that AA meeting, the one in the legion hall, the one you quit after week two, the one you should probably go back to, if for nothing else than to make a last ditch attempt at not feeling like a total wreck at work every morning.

Your grandma has switched the tune to Thriller. The claws emerge.

You've made it to the window seat. You're standing in front of Phil. Phil sees you. He sets down Colonel Mustard and Mrs. Peacock to shake your hand. You reconsider the coup. You're only at the handshaking stage. There's still time to abort your mission. There's still time to admit to yourself that your enthusiasm to turn in your grandmother is largely driven by the desire to let someone else be the screw-up for a change, so you can feel a foot taller than usual, or at the very least, make someone else feel a foot shorter.

But, you open your mouth, and there's no turning back now. You tell Phil that you have to tell him something, and Phil nods to indicate he's ready to hear the something. You glance over your shoulder for a second.

Knobby elbows are at right angles. Faces are contorted to look like hissing cats. The beasts are turning at the waist, twisting in their seats over reconstructed hips whilst lip syncing to the King of Pop. The retired patent attorney has fashioned a sling out of his windbreaker to continue dancing.

You tell Phil your grandma is the one who has been stealing the tomatoes from the front yard. Phil closes his eyes. The news appears to have disappointed Phil far more than you had anticipated. You shake your head in shame and offer to pay for new tomatoes and new seeds and even new boxes, and Phil raises a finger. He must be really upset, you think, but just when you're in the middle of offering him a lump sum for the crime, he shushes you. You fall silent. Phil isn't pissed about the tomatoes; he's pissed at you. You just had to ruin it, he says.

You blink. Phil isn't looking at you anymore. He's frowning at the geriatric mosh pit doing jazz hands. You ask what you ruined.

Phil knew she was stealing the tomatoes. He knew the whole time. You see, Phil goes grocery shopping for everyone at Sunset Valley, and your grandma has never ordered a tomato in seven years. Not a one. But she heard Phil talk about Sicily. She was sitting on her couch at the time, watching Ellen while Phil knelt down by the coffee table and counted her tabs of lisinopril, and Phil noticed Sophia Loren was on the television, and he asked your grandma if she had ever been to Italy, and when she returned the question to Phil, and he said no, the subsequent back-and-forth eventually yanked out a nervous laugh from Phil, along with a confession that he'd always wanted to go to Sicily. For the pasta. No, the sauce; the pasta the seniors made in their classes was pretty good. But what did it matter now? The opiates had put Phil in debt worth seven trips to Sicily.

So, when Phil found the mason jar of homemade pasta sauce in his little cubby in the breakroom, who else could he suspect? But that's not what's important right now.

What's important is for you to look at the sign near the door that Phil is pointing at. And you look, you do, you squint at the sign, the sign by the door you walked through just minutes earlier. It's a safety sign, a sign for safety, a sign exhorting safety, with step-by-step instructions for evacuating the building, replete with little cartoon people leading even littler cartoon old people by the arm as a fire rages in the background.

Phil tells you he has exactly zero experience helping old people out of burning buildings, but, guess what, that sign is fireproof, and you know why it's fireproof? So that, in the event of a fire, the owner of Sunset Valley can pull that sign up out of the ashes of burnt carpet and jazz hands and say, See, I cared.

Phil's father wasn't too different from the owner of Sunset Valley, because Phil's father bought a De Beers for Phil's mom, but that didn't stop him from meeting up with hookers every weekend at a motel downtown.

And Phil's brother Steve might have a little bit of the owner of Sunset Valley inside him too, because Steve once said he'd love Phil No Matter What, Brother, but where was Steve when Phil was in jail for lifting oxy?

And aren't we all like that, Phil wonders aloud, so focused on ourselves, that even when we do something nice, we're more concerned with broadcasting our virtues and love and selflessness than we are with actually delivering? But not your grandma. She had the mind to remove herself from the equation entirely. And unlike the safety sign or the De Beers or Steve's empty promise, that jar of pasta sauce was pure. No note, no credit, no handoff with a self-indulgent twinkle in her eye that said, Look what a nice person I am. Just garlic, olive oil, and tomatoes.

Phil resumes picking up the game of Clue. The song on the cassette player has changed to Beat It. Even in sitting positions, the hip thrusts are impressive.

You know when it's your cue to leave. You slip out of the room and drag yourself back to the front door. It's raining outside. You push through the double doors and leave the warmth of the lobby behind you. You walk under the awning, but before you reach the end of the path, you steal a glance at the box of tomatoes hanging from the ground floor window.

You get a wild idea. You rush back into the building and steal an umbrella from the rack by the door, and as you run out into the downpour, you can't quite believe what you're doing, but you mustn't get wet, you absolutely mustn't get wet, and when you reach the tomato box, you steal a fat one—it isn't important that it's fat, it just worked out that way—and now you're back inside, tossing the umbrella back in the rack, running so fast you hardly notice the tropical climate on your way to the mailboxes.

And then you stop. Because there are so many mailboxes, two hundred of them, all rectangular holes in the wall protected only by the honor system. You find your grandma's box and pause to look yourself over once more. You're dry. Not a drop to drip. You place the tomato in her mailbox and run for the exercise room. You stop outside to catch your breath.

And then you walk in. Everything is more or less just as you left it—Phil is still picking up the game of clue; your grandma is still conducting the hand-waving cult; the cult members are all still entranced. As the song changes to Human Nature, you lean up against the wall and rest. Eventually, your grandma will come up and ask to what she owes the honor of your visit. And you'll say you're just here if anyone needs a partner in bridge. She'll be skeptical, and that will be fine. You needn't say any more. You're just here to play bridge. That's all she needs to know.

A GUY WITH A BRITISH ACCENT

Going into the third year of my relationship with Martha, I decided to tell her I did not actually have a British accent. For the record, it was not because I slipped up. Ever. I did not spend years watching the BBC to let that happen. And I didn't decide to tell her the truth because any of my friends or family members had slipped up either. The actors I hired were professionals and they all gave terrific performances.

For example, at my fake father's fake funeral, Martha asked if we could open up the casket so she could return the cherished locket my fake father, Bo, had given to her for her thirtieth birthday. The only issue was that the casket was empty. So, naturally, we ushered Martha out of the room and distracted her while we called up Bo, who was about to go into an audition in North Hollywood. He kept us waiting for at least an hour and a half because the 405 was a nightmare, and when he finally arrived we had to get six of my fake cousins to all pitch in to squeeze Bo's big ass into the casket while Martha was two rooms away meeting with the psychic I hired.

"I can hear Bo talking to me from the afterlife," the psychic told Martha, which was kind of true, because Bo was on the other side of the wall yelling at my fake cousins, 'Just give it up, you bastards, I don't fit!'

And the psychic said, "There he is now."

And Martha said, "Oh my God, I think I hear him too," and Bo yelled out something like, 'For God's sake, you can't use a folding chair to try to shoe-horn me into this thing; just get a stiff piece of construction paper and lubricate my sides with soap.'

And Martha said, "God, I hope he's not in pain."

And the psychic said, "No, no, there's no pain in the afterlife. Why don't we go take this little séance into the garden?"

And Bo screamed, "I will not keep my voice down when I'm getting manhandled by six primates trying to stuff me into a coffin."

Anyway, the reason why I decided to tell Martha the truth about my fake

British accent is because trust is the foundation of every relationship.

"Bullshit," Fogler said, so loudly that a few people in the diner stared at us.

I was a little taken aback. Sure, Fogler was only my fake best friend, but over the years, he had definitely earned a spot among my top seven to eight real friends in LA county, and I expected everyone in my top ten to support me.

"No, I'm serious," I said. "That's why I'm telling her."

"I believe you," Fogler said, wiping egg off his mouth, "I just don't believe trust is the foundation of a relationship." He unbuttoned his shirt a few buttons and looked out the window. "And did you say every relationship? Un-uh." He narrowed his eyes at a squirrel crossing the street. We both watched as a passing semi-truck flattened it against the pavement. "Shame," Fogler said, and he rested his elbows on the table. "Look, relationships are built on one thing and one thing only." He paused, pointing his finger at me like a gun.

"What?"

"Intrigue," he said, and spun around in his seat. "Lisa!" he hollered over his shoulder.

Our waitress ambled over cautiously. "Yes?"

Fogler started stacking all our plates. "We, my colleague and I, are going to need that check."

Lisa tore it off and set it on our table. "Whenever you're ready," she said, and started walking away.

"Well now, hold up," Fogler said, putting his hand up. "Let's talk about it."

Lisa paused. "Okay."

Fogler pointed at his empty plate. "These eggs."

Lisa's eyebrows slowly floated up her forehead. "Yes?"

"Goddamn beautiful."

"I'm so glad."

Fogler gestured out the window with his thumb. "But on the contraire, you're going to want to take a spatula and a bus tub out to the street right there."

"What?" Lisa said.

Fogler dropped his napkin on the table. "Yeah, there's a squirrel out there flat as a crepe. Don't get me wrong, he almost made it to the sidewalk. And if he had? Who knows. Maybe meet a nice lady squirrel? Move to Pasadena. Start a family. But we'll never know now, right? Ha. No, we'll never know. But that's okay. That's common. Another missed opportunity. What's uncommon is the man who actually gets to the sidewalk. Walks in here. Orders eggs. Musters up the courage to tell his waitress she looks like a tulip on an April afternoon. Invites her to a pottery making class on a sailboat. Steady hands. Steady feet. Watch for the boom. Takes her on a couple of beach cruisers to a picnic blanket on top of a grassy hill with a view of the ocean. Chardonnay and ceviche. Bon appetit."

I offered my credit card to Lisa.

To my surprise, she didn't take it. She was too busy staring, open-mouthed, at Fogler as if he had just pulled off a mask to reveal that, underneath this human-like facade, he was actually an octopus.

"I'm free after one on Saturday," she said quietly. Then she turned on her heel and walked away.

Fogler grinned at me. He knocked against the table. "See?" he said. "Intrigue."

***

When I told my fake father, Bo, what happened with Fogler, he was horrified.

"I'm so sorry," Bo told me. "Fogler knows nothing about women."

"But that's the weird thing," I said. "The waitress wanted to go on the date with him."

Bo waved me off. "Everyone gets lucky."

"So you don't think intrigue is the foundation of every relationship?"

"No," Bo said. "That's ridiculous. Forgiveness is the foundation of every relationship." He toasted me with his Manhattan and sat back on his couch. "That and the occasional back rub. Right honey?"

His wife, Beatrice, laughed from the den. "Right-o!"

I let out a sigh of relief. "So I can come clean to Martha about not having a British accent?"

Bo choked on his drink and shook his head. "No, you need to keep that going."

I nearly spilled my John Collins. "Bo, you said forgiveness is the foundation of every relationship."

"Did I?" Bo said, sipping. He busied himself with a coaster. "Maybe for most people."

"But not for me?"

Bo froze. He tossed the coaster aside and poked at his ice cubes with his straw. "Roger, I'm going to be very frank with you. Martha is beautiful. And you are hideous."

"What?"

"And you have a tinny voice."

"Bo."

"And you have the personality of a jellyfish."

"I don't even know what that means."

"You're a soft squishy invertebrate." Bo downed the rest of his

Manhattan and chewed on the ice. His eyes narrowed as he stared at me. "But when you speak in that British accent…" Bo swallowed his ice and looked longingly at the ceiling. "Roger, I've never told you this before—and I say this as a man who has never thought about another man sexually—but sometimes when I'm making love to my wife, I think about your British accent."

"Just the accent?"

Bo nodded. "It's like the first time I tasted nutella."

Bo's wife came into the room and rested her hand on his shoulder.

"Beatrice," Bo said without looking back, "I didn't mean for you to hear that."

"It's okay," Beatrice said, staring at me. "I think about his accent too."

***

When I got home, I started getting dressed for the evening. Martha and I were going to a British murder mystery party where we all had to be in costume. I was assigned the role of the butler.

As I put on my dark trousers, and buttoned up my starched white shirt, I thought about my conversations with Bo and Fogler. Was forgiveness the foundation of every relationship? Or was it intrigue? And what did this mean for my fake British accent?

As Martha drove us to the party, I tried to come clean to her.

"Martha," I said, "there's something I've been meaning to tell you."

"What is it?" she said, turning the wheel. She pulled up to the curb of a Holiday Inn.

"Wait," I said, "is the party at a Holiday Inn? I thought it was at Sophia's house."

A middle-aged couple dressed in 1950s cocktail attire approached our car.

"Are those your parents?" I said.

Martha grabbed my arm. "Surprise," she said. "They're so excited to see you."

Martha's father, Wilson, opened the passenger door and gave me a big hug. "There's my favorite British chap! Come here you bloody old bloke! Blimey!"

"Hi, Roger," Martha's mother, Phyllis, said. She blew me a kiss and gave me a finger wiggling wave.

After we pulled away from the curb, Martha turned on some smooth jazz. "A little Humphrey Lyttleton to set the mood," she said. She winked at me. "Did you know he was born in Buckinghamshire? Just like you, Roger."

***

Sophia answered the door in a red cocktail dress.

"I got lipstick on you," she said after she kissed me on the cheek. She took out a hankie and dabbed at my face. "Oh, it's not coming off," she said. Sophia, who was actually British, always put me on high alert. I researched my fake hometown for over fifteen hours last week.

"Quite all right," I said. "I'll just go to the loo."

"The loo!" Phyllis said, clutching Wilson's arm.

"I'll take you," Sophia said, and she whisked me past a cluster of chatting people in the hallway. "There is someone you simply must meet," Sophia told me. "His name is Mr. Wishmail."

Mr. Wishmail turned out to be Bo in a three-piece suit and a top hat. We caught him in the middle of a conversation with Fogler.

"I have some more guests at the door," Sophia said, tossing her head back as she floated away. "Loo's over there. Ciao!"

I turned to Bo and Fogler.

"Cheerful, that one," Bo said.

"You're supposed to be dead," I said. "And you're supposed to be in Panama!" I said to Fogler. "You guys need to get out of here."

"We have just as much of a right to be here as you," Bo said. He threw back his cocktail. "If you want to hire me as an actor, you know my hourly rate."

Martha and her parents began to emerge from the hallway. I dragged Bo into the library and sat him down by the fireplace. "What do you want?" I said.

"A Manhattan."

"Done."

I returned to the bar area to find Martha and her parents chatting with Fogler.

"So the plane crashed in the jungle?" Wilson said.

"Right into a thicket of bombacopsis," Fogler said. "If it weren't for the caravan going by, I'd still be wandering around out there."

"And what was it like crossing the border?" Phyllis said.

"Just a quick swim across the Rio Grande," Fogler said. "Walking back to Los Angeles was the hard part."

"Ladies and gentlemen!" Sophia called out. She was standing on a chair to speak over the crowd. "Mr. Chanksworth has been murdered!"

***

I read over my instruction card.

BUTLER

Personality: proper, polite, obedient.

NOTES:

Talk to Mrs. Lanning. She has something to give you.
Look upstairs in the office.
Mrs. Filbert has a secret for you.
Don't trust Mr. Portmill.

I tossed my instruction card in the trash and grabbed Bo by the collar.

"You have to get out of here," I said, dragging him toward the back door.

"But I need to talk to Mr. Portmill," Bo said, reading his card.

"Don't bother."

Bo turned around and put his hands on my shoulders. "Roger, relax. Sophia has a costume box everyone was grabbing from. I'm sure I can find a fake beard or one of those pairs of glasses with the nose."

"You're supposed to be dead!" I said. "Martha's known you for over two years. Do you really think you can fool her?"

"It's a huge house. I probably won't even run into her." He looked over my shoulder. "Here's Sophia now," Bo said. "Sophia, love!"

"I have something to give you," Sophia told me. I flinched as she put something in my back pocket. "By the way," she said, whispering in my ear. "I don't know too many people from Buckinghamshire with Yorkshire accents."

"Traveled there as a kid," I said.

"And to Australia too?" she said. She smirked and walked away.

When I turned back to Bo, he had disappeared.

***

Bo was nowhere to be found on the ground floor, so I walked upstairs.

"Bo," I called out, pushing through some French doors. I was in Sophia's office. I could see the Pacific Ocean outside of her bay windows. And in front of the windows: an oak desk with a small wooden box.

I patted my back pocket and found the key. It fit perfectly into the box's heart shaped lock. The latch clicked open.

Inside was a photograph of Martha and me at a tea shop on our first date. It was the date where I made the fateful error of saying, "Pleasure to meet you" in a British accent because I was so nervous my brain momentarily broke.

"Oi," said a voice behind me. "There he is." It was Martha. She smirked at me as she raised a magnifying glass to her eye. "So it was the butler."

***

We took the stairs to the rooftop and sat in the cabana facing the ocean.

"How long have you known?" I said.

"A few months," Martha said, shivering.

I wrapped my butler jacket around her shoulders. "Did I mispronounce something?"

She shook her head. "I saw Bo in a sushi restaurant."

"Ah."

"He was drunk on Sapporo. Seemed upset you'd killed off his character."

I watched the waves crash into the Malibu cliffs. "And this is why I had to kill him," I muttered under my breath.

"What?"

"Nothing," I said. I turned back to Martha and held her hands in mine. "Martha, I am so sorry. So very very sorry. I was planning on telling you. Tonight, actually."

"I know."

My eyebrows jumped up my forehead. "You knew?"

She nodded. "I tracked down Fogler and twisted his arm until he told me everything." She had a mischievous smile on her face.

"Must have taken about five seconds."

"I twist hard," she said. Then she took the picture of us on our first date out of her pocket and set it on my knee. I stared at our slightly younger selves smiling next to a tray of biscuits. "You didn't have to do this, you know," she said.

"I know."

"You could have just been yourself."

"I know that now."

"But it shouldn't have taken you three years to learn that," she said.

I hung my head. Then I looked back up at her. Our eyes locked together, mirroring each other's sadness. I squeezed her hand. "Do you forgive me?"

"No," she said.

I nodded. "I understand. I just hope—"

"I'm breaking up with you," she said.

In the canyon below, a wave crested and curled in on itself, rumbling against the cliff wall.

"You lied to me for three years," Martha said. "You hired actors to trick me. You held funerals for your fake parents. I never cared about the accent, Roger."

Martha stood up from the plush white cushion and walked to the stairs. She opened the door, took the first step down, and then paused with her hand on the railing, her eyes on the floor.

"But there's good in you too," she said. "I'd like to think that was real." She looked up at me. A strand of hair fluttered against her face as she frowned. "Call me in three months. As the American Roger. Ask me out on a first date. See if I respond."

She closed the door.

TOPHER

In the middle of reading Goodnight Moon to his class of two dozen five-year-olds, Topher Schmidt shut the book and said the government faked the moon landing.

Two pages into Oh, the Places You'll Go!, Topher said ambition was futile, travel was meaningless, and everyone we ever cared about would eventually die.

Four pages into Alexander and the Terrible, Horrible, No Good, Very Bad Day, he claimed the moral of the story was that God does not exist, true love is a myth, and we are all a bunch of cells on a spinning rock flying through a pointless universe towards oblivion.

And when the kids played Hungry Hungry Hippos, Topher stopped the game and said, "Yes. The hippos. They are hungry, aren't they? Striving. Reaching. Yearning for meaning. Yet life will never satiate their endless desires. And then they will die. Cold, tired, and alone."

It's only when the kids are finger painting that Topher has anything positive to say. He'll stare at the kids' paintings, examining every detail of the smeared colors on printer paper. "Yes," he'll say. "That is art." Then he'll go outside and look off into the distance while he chain smokes cigarettes.

I have only been teaching kindergarten for three weeks. Topher and I have been paired to teach together for the next eight and a half months.

I have to do something about Topher.

***

I start by meeting with the principal, Mrs. Grieves. She is ninety-seven years old and has the sensory perception of an earthworm, a fact which surely played a role in her decision to hire Topher. I meet with the human relic in her office while the kids are in music class.

"Mrs. Grieves?" I say as I walk in.

She continues writing a note on her desk.

"Mrs. Grieves?"

She breaks her pencil and looks up at me. "Oh hi, Bobby, how are you?" she says. Her smile sparkles with kindness. She smells like freshly baked cookies.

"Mrs. Grieves, I want to talk to you about Topher."

"Yes?"

I clear my throat to start reciting the lines I practiced in the mirror this morning, but abandon them in favor of something simpler. "Topher is a complete disaster."

Mrs. Grieves interrupts me. "Bobby," she says in a scolding tone, "we do not gossip in this school."

"I'm not gossiping, Mrs. Grieves," I say. "I'm filing a formal complaint. Did you not hear what Topher said after Petey the hamster died?"

She looks down at her notes, but she isn't reading. "Death is a difficult subject to explain to children."

"He said Petey is in purgatory. He said Petey never made significant strides in improving his character, and he'll be lucky to return to earth as a preying mantis."

Mrs. Grieves holds up her hands. "I'm not one to criticize the religious beliefs of others—"

I lose my temper. "He said Billy will never be an astronaut! He said sixty percent of everyone's parents will divorce! He said there is no reality, no truth, no meaning, and for God's sake, Petey the hamster would still be alive if Topher hadn't let him out of his cage next to the Jenga game!"

Mrs. Grieves points a warning finger at me. "Topher is passionate about animal freedom."

"But he's not passionate about making kids happy!"

"It is not our job to make kids happy," Mrs. Grieves says. "It is our job to teach. It is our job to prepare our pupils for life. And life isn't always pretty, Bobby." She pushes her reading glasses further up on the bridge of her nose and flips a few pages on her desk. "In fact, I'm a little concerned about your teaching methods. A parent called last week to complain that you led the kids in some sort of ritual chant about wheels on a bus?" She checks her notes. "Something about the 'wheels going round and round?'"

"Yes," I say.

Mrs. Grieves scowls at me. "We're not teaching kids to be car mechanics, Bobby. We're giving them a solid foundation in the liberal arts. It's about time you learned that."

Later that day, I'm driving home furiously in my Volkswagen Beetle. "About time I learned that, huh?" I say to my windshield.

When I get back to my cottage, I make chicken soup from a can. I light some candles, draw myself a bath, and I read Stuart Little. Then, I put on my Thomas the Tank Engine pajamas and crawl into my race car bed. Two hours after I turn out the lights, I'm still staring at the glow-in-the-dark stars on my ceiling.

I really have to do something about Topher.

***

The next day, I stand next to Mrs. Barrett at recess. Mrs. Barrett is one of our parent volunteers. Today, she helped the kids cut out turkey handprints. It's only ten a.m., but Mrs. Barrett already smells strongly of cheap vodka.

"Did you enjoy the lesson, Mrs. Barrett?" I say as I approach her.

She coughs and stuffs her flask in her pocket. I've startled her. "Yes, well, it's hard to mess up handprints," she says.

Indeed. I clasp my hands behind my back and squint at the children on the playground. They're climbing the jungle gym, going down the slide, running around in circles shouting nonsense. I can see Mrs. Barrett looking at me nervously. She's thumbing the flask in her pocket. "Are you looking forward to the afternoon lesson?" I ask her. I glance at her casually. "With Topher."

Her face softens. "Oh, yes. He's so practical! Billy used to come home all the time talking about being an astronaut, but Topher set him straight. Now Billy wants to be a philosopher. His father isn't thrilled about it, but his father's a cheating bastard, so what does he know?"

Mrs. Barrett either doesn't realize she is taking a sip from her flask, or no longer cares if I see.

"Did you hear what Topher said about Petey the hamster?" I say.

"Oh, was that insightful or what?" Mrs. Barrett marvels as she screws on the cap. "Billy's father said Petey is in a better place. Ha! Maybe I should scoop him up with a shovel and toss him out in the woods!"

I try to look like I'm concentrating on a game of hopscotch.

Mrs. Barrett licks her pinky and starts polishing her flask. "So, does, uh, Topher have a girlfriend?" she says. "Asking for a friend."

***

At lunchtime, I talk to another mom and a stay-at-home dad, but neither are on my side. They tell me they love Topher. All the parents love him. I talk to the vice-principals, and then to the other teachers. Nothing. Everyone loves Topher.

Everyone except for Charlotte Penny.

Charlotte is another kindergarten teacher. She was hired at the same time that Topher and I were, and to my delight, she hates him.

"I hate that guy," she tells me in the teacher's lounge.

I am hopelessly in love with Charlotte Penny.

"He's so jaded!" Charlotte says as she takes an angry bite of an English muffin. "I mean, is he trying to ruin kindergarten?" Charlotte looks adorable as she fumes at the table. She's wearing a sunflower dress that lights up her blue eyes. Her auburn hair is pulled back in a tight bun. She has a Mickey Mouse watch and a locket with a picture of her cat inside.

I want to marry Charlotte Penny.

"He is jaded," I say, "but everyone loves him, Charlotte. They say he's the future of kindergarten. They'll never fire him."

"Then we need to destroy him," Charlotte says. Her eyes get wide as she chews on her muffin.

"Destroy him?" I say cautiously. I have suddenly become a little afraid of Charlotte Penny. "Destroy him how, exactly?"

Charlotte stands and walks to the corkboard covered with adverts for field trip fundraisers and tee ball tryouts. She rips off an orange page with brown font and hands it to me. "The fall recital on Saturday." She says, and she looks down at me while I read the flyer. "For three hours, a hundred parents will be held captive in the auditorium while the kids sing songs about pilgrims and Native Americans."

I look up. "Yeah, so?"

Charlotte grins. "Topher does spoken word poetry, right?"

"I think so."

Charlotte taps the flyer. "If we let Topher perform in front of every parent in the school, there are bound to be complaints."

"There haven't been any yet."

"That's because no one has heard Topher say more than a paragraph. But if we give him twenty minutes to go full unhinged Debbie Downer on everyone, he'll get fired for sure." Charlotte taps the flyer again. "You just have to get him up on stage."

***

The next day, I show up to our classroom at seven a.m. sharp. The first kid won't arrive for at least another twenty minutes. The timing is perfect.

I find Topher at the window, staring at something with his binoculars. He is almost unrecognizable. The black sweater and skinny black jeans he wears daily have been replaced by a blue gingham shirt tucked into chinos. His black combat boots have been switched out for loafers. He's wearing a watch. I cross the room and ask him what he's looking at.

"I think it's an owl's nest," he says. "Up in that cedar tree over there?" He points as he hands me the binoculars. "A barn owl I think. Maybe a

Great Horned or a Boreal." He looks childlike sitting on the window seat with his legs tucked up underneath him.

I raise the binoculars to my face. "They sometimes eat their young, don't they?" I say, explaining aloud why I think Topher is owl-watching.

"Do they?" he says. With the binoculars over my eyes, I can't see him, but he sounds genuinely surprised. "I hope not. I wanted to show the kids."

It takes me a few seconds to locate the nest. It looks like a leaf pile perched on a thatched floor of branches. Just as I'm about to hand the binoculars back to Topher, the leaves rustle, and a head pops up. "That's not an owl's nest," I say. I can hear Topher press his palms against the window. "That's a squirrel." I hand him back the binoculars.

"Wow! Incredible!" he says as he takes a look through the binoculars. He reaches out blindly and pats me on the shoulder. "Good find, Bobby. Did you know squirrels play a vital role in the ecosystem?"

I stare at him.

"It's true," he says. "If squirrels didn't spread seeds around, we wouldn't see the abundance of trees we see today. Pine, Birch, Oak, Chestnut—all of them rely on the squirrel." He starts pointing excitedly. "Oh! Oh! And look at the truffles on that cedar! Did you know squirrels eat the mushrooms and poop their spores around the forest? And the mushrooms pull in water and nutrients that help the trees grow. Isn't that remarkable? It's like this whole system where everyone contributes and helps each other out."

I continue to stare at Topher.

"Are you okay?" I say.

He's looking through the binoculars again. "Yeah, I mean, I wish it were an owl's nest, but then again, if the owls are eating their young—"

"No, seriously," I say. "What happened?"

Topher lowers the binoculars. He's still facing the window. "Was it that obvious?"

I choose not to respond.

"Allen died," he says. He looks vacantly over my shoulder. "I thought Mrs. Barrett told you."

I look left and see a black dog leash hanging on the coat rack. Topher would use the leash to tie up his massive Great Dane outside, but I haven't seen the dog in at least a week. "I'm sorry," I say.

Topher nods and raises the binoculars back to his eyes.

We both jump when our brightest student, Sally, comes through the front door. It's raining outside, and her pink raincoat is wet. "Get the towels from the cubbies," she says, sighing. Sally is one of those shockingly responsible children who was essentially born middle-aged. "You know someone is going to forget an umbrella," Sally says as she hangs up her coat. She sighs again. "Mrs. Barrett, probably."

***

"His dog died?" Charlotte Penny says. I'm in her cottage, seated at her circular dining room table. Her hands shake as she tears open a tea bag. "I don't believe it."

"Believe it," I say. "I don't know if the dog was just old or the beast got hit by a car but—"

"That's not what I meant," Charlotte snaps. In the dim lamplight of her tiny kitchen, she looks stunningly cute. "I mean, I don't believe he's really changed."

"Oh he's changed, all right," I say as I help myself to one of the homemade snickerdoodles on the table. "He was talking about squirrels and mushrooms and how we all need to team up to save the trees or something—I don't remember the details, but it was really uplifting stuff, Charlotte."

She frowns as she serves the tea. "And the dog was, what, holding him hostage this whole time? And the tyranny just ended?"

I shrug.

She flattens her dress before sitting down. "Well, it's going to take a little more than a squirrel story to redeem him, don't you think?" She almost seems disappointed. I sense some feeling of loss in her voice, a missed opportunity—for schadenfreude, perhaps.

"I don't know," I say. I stir my tea and get lost in the little whirlpool for a moment. "This whole day he seemed different. He asked what everyone was fingerpainting, and oohed and aahed. He didn't change the lyrics to any of the songs. And he read books—entire books! And he didn't insert his own moral of the story anywhere."

Charlotte still seems incredulous. She snatches up a snickerdoodle compulsively and bites into it. "I talked to Mrs. Grieves today."

I sip my tea.

"I told her we should have Topher read his poetry at the fall recital tomorrow."

I continue to sip my tea.

"She loved the idea." The corner of Charlotte's mouth curls into a smile. A few crumbs fall to the table. "She said she's personally going to invite Topher." Charlotte's smile widens—if she isn't careful, it will turn into a full-blown evil grin. "She thinks we could turn the recital into a fundraiser. Poetry, music, dancing, maybe even an open bar for the parents. We'd cut the kids' singing down to about fifteen minutes."

"Sounds like a big event," I say.

"Exactly," she says, and she points at me. "Huge. We'll have to move the whole thing into the gym. You know how many people can fit into that gym?" Charlotte leans forward. A folded corner of her dress dips into her tea, but she doesn't notice. "Five hundred," she says. She leans back and nods.

"That's a lot of people," I say.

"A lot of people," she says. She grabs a flyer off the counter and slaps it on the table in front of me. "Can you help me set up tomorrow?"

I look down at the flyer.

I take another bite of cookie.

I am still hopelessly in love with Charlotte Penny.

***

When I wake up on Saturday, it takes me an hour to get out of bed. When I finally do, I eat Sour Patch Kids cereal with a spoon that looks like an airplane. I brush my teeth with my smiling leprechaun toothbrush. I take a long walk around the pond behind my cottage and feed the tadpoles with some leftover cereal from breakfast. I watch with horror as one of the tadpoles goes belly-up.

I do not have a history of ruining people's careers, and it eats away at my conscience to think I might start today. I think about Topher the entire drive to school, and I continue thinking about him as I help Charlotte and Mrs. Grieves set up the gym for the Fall Recital. It's just the three of us, but I still feel the presence of our colleague.

I imagine New Topher walking through the gym doors, smiling and waving at us cheerfully, his dress shirt freshly ironed, his slacks freshly pressed.

I also imagine Old Topher walking in with his usual outfit—black boots, black shirt, black jeans. I picture him extinguishing a cigarette on his leather bracelet while he scrutinizes one of the turkey handprints we're hanging up on the stage. "Turkeys," he would say. "The most conscious type of poultry."

I pray he doesn't show.

***

By two p.m., every bleacher in the gym is packed with parents, grandparents, and siblings in wet coats. Their faces are sullen. They want to be entertained. They quiet down when Charlotte leads a train of little pilgrims and Native Americans onto the stage. I watch from my corner backstage, peeking around the curtain.

"Welcome," she says into the microphone as she takes a seat at the piano, "to the Fall Recital."

Then she starts playing a naively upbeat little number on the piano and the kids start singing. Many of the fathers in the audience look down at their phones.

During the last song of the performance, one of the pilgrims pukes on a Native American, and a voice behind me says, "It's good what we're doing here."

I turn around. It's Topher.

I let go of the curtain. "What—um—what are we doing here?" I say, not entirely of my own volition.

"Giving thanks," he says. He inhales appreciatively. "There's nothing quite like the sound of children singing."

I inspect his outfit. He's dressed in loafers, chinos, a black turtleneck, and a black beret. I am not sure which Topher has shown up, but I cannot risk it. My conscience weighs on me. "Listen, Topher," I say. "I wanted to talk to you. About your poetry."

Topher smiles as he watches Mrs. Grieves escort the puke-covered Native American off the stage. "I have a tough act to follow, don't I?"

I falter. "Sure. But, look, you've been through a lot, and I'm just not sure this event is the best event for you to express yourself...poetically."

He blinks at me. I can hear the kids onstage wrapping up their song. "I don't understand," he says.

"Well," I say, laughing nervously, "I was just thinking about what you told me yesterday about Allen dying and such, and—gosh, you've been through a lot."

He continues to stare at me, puzzled. "I'm going to talk about Allen. In my poetry."

"That's what I'm worried about," I say. I can hear the audience applauding. The kids have finished their last song.

Topher smiles at me. "Nothing to worry about," he says, and he makes a move for the curtain.

I grab his arm before he can go onstage. "Topher, I don't know if that dog bit you, or barked all night, or just pooped all over your house, but," I say earnestly, "people are going to be a little freaked out if you sound like you're happy your dog died."

Topher pauses to watch Mrs. Grieves lead the kids off the stage to a section of chairs near their parents. "Bobby, I don't know what you're talking about," Topher says.

"You've changed," I say, pointing at him. "For the first three weeks of the school year, you filled the kids' heads with nihilist propaganda. But ever since your dog Allen died, you're Mister Positive."

Topher cocks his head to the side. "Allen died three weeks ago," Topher says. "And he's not my dog."

"Up next," Charlotte says in a cheery voice from the other side of the curtain, "we have a poetry reading from our very own Topher Schmidt."

Topher walks onstage. I briefly make eye contact with Charlotte. She smiles at me. The lights dim, bathing us in darkness.

***

For a moment, the only sound in the gym is the click of Topher's dress shoes on the hollow stage floor. A spotlight turns on, illuminating a lone wooden stool and a microphone. Topher sits down and pulls the mic stand closer to him. He breathes into it softly. The audience of hundreds falls silent.

"This first poem is called 'I Heard They Eat Their Young,'" he says. "By Topher Schmidt and Bobby Bailey." He lowers his gaze to the index cards in his lap and begins reading.

"'Look, an owl's nest,' I say as I look through my binoculars with the innocence of a child. 'I heard they eat their young,' says my best friend and fellow kindergarten teacher, Bobby Bailey. 'I hope not,' I say. 'I was hoping to show the kids.'"

I draw the curtain a little further across my body.

Topher flips to the next index card. "This next poem," he says, "is called 'From the Bowels of Owls.' By Topher Schmidt." Topher takes a deep breath.

"Cracked metatarsals. Scapula stripped and splintered. Humerus. Femurs. Ribs. Cleft cartilage from the calf of an undulate? No. It is vermin vertebrae twisted in the excrement of an owl. What I have dissected is the digested, disintegrating, defunct corpse of the deceased. 'But what about the dreams of a little squirrel?' you might ask. Simple. The varmint's ambitions have evaporated from the shell of its cracked skull."

Topher flips to the next index card. "This next poem is called 'Snapped in the Grip of Talons.' By Topher Schmidt.

"The squirrel let out a scream as the owl ripped the varmint out of its burrow. The owl fed the squirrel to its chicks, some of whom were eaten by the owl mother, and some of whom grew up only to be eaten by an eagle. The eagle was shot by a hunter. The hunter got lost in the woods and died of dysentery."

Topher takes the top index card and neatly inserts it in the back of the deck. "This next poem is called 'Allen.'" He clears his throat. "By Topher Schmidt." He pauses.

"The month is July. The year is this year. I'm walking into St. Jude's Hospital with a bouquet of flowers in my hand. The nurses and doctors and orderlies all know me here. I have been here at all times—day and night—and all the staff members of every shift recognize me. They look at me sympathetically. I nod as I pass them in the hallways. When I enter Allen's room, he is completely supine, staring up at the ceiling while a machine—to which he is connected by at least a half-dozen tubes—beeps.

"'Allen,' I say. 'It's Topher.'

"At first, I think that he is so sedated, he does not recognize me, but after a few seconds, he pulls the oxygen mask off his face and says, 'Topher? Is that you?'"

"'Yes," I say, and take his hand. "Yes, Allen, I'm here."

"'Topher,' he says, 'I have to tell you something. But I don't have much time before the drugs in my system sedate me again.'

"And I say, 'I'm here, Allen. I'm listening.'

"And he says, "I want you to promise me something, Topher.'

"And I say, 'Anything, Allen. What do you need?'

"And he says, 'You are a ray of sunshine in an otherwise dark world. Even in my worst moments, you cheered me up. At a time when life seemed so ugly, you showed me life was beautiful.' Allen squeezes my hand and sits up a little so he can look me in the eye. 'I know you're going to start teaching kindergarten in September…'"

"'Yes,' I say.

"'Show these kids what you showed me: that life is beautiful, Topher.' He sits back and looks up at the ceiling. The drugs are slowly kicking in. His eyes are glazing over. 'Life is beautiful,' he says one last time, and his voice trails off."

Topher looks up from his notes. "Miraculously," he says to the crowd, "Allen made a full recovery."

He looks back down at his index cards. "So, I go to Allen's house to celebrate his recovery, and we drink champagne and toast to his health, and then I say, 'Allen, you better open your present.' And he says, 'Topher, you didn't need to get me a present!' And I say, 'Don't be silly. You literally almost died.' So he goes, 'Okay, if you insist. Where is it?' And I say, 'Let me go get it.' And so then I do, and I come back with this long cardboard tube—you know, the kind you stick posters in—but this one's wriggling around, and Allen says, 'What the hell is this?' And I say, 'Just open it!' And he says, 'No seriously, is this an animal? I think it's trying to get out.' And I say, 'Just open it, silly!' And he says, 'It's shrieking. And it smells really bad.' And it takes like frickin' forever for Allen to open his present because it keeps fighting, but he finally does, and when he does, he closes the tube and gives me this dopey surprised look and says, 'Topher what is this.' And I say, 'Well, Allen, after you beat your terminal illness, it only made sense for me to give you the squirrel I found in my attic who beat his own terminal illnesses. The vet said this little guy had all kinds of things. You see, Allen, this little squirrel is just like you. Guess what I named him!' And he says, 'What?' And I say, 'Allen.' And he looks up and says, 'I love it.'

"So we go out in the back yard to walk it. And I have my dog Nietzsche on a leash and Allen the human has Allen the squirrel on a leash and we're all walking around in the woods laughing at how much Allen the squirrel tugs on his leash, and I say, 'What a handful, right?' And Allen the human laughs. And I'm telling Allen the human everything I've learned about squirrels from reading about them the night before I bought Allen the squirrel, and I'm telling Allen the human about how smart they are and how they're really good at escaping their cages, and how it's, like, super dangerous to sleep in the same room with one, but even though you have to take some precautions to make sure your pet squirrel doesn't gnaw your face off while you're sleeping, you never, ever, ever have to worry about this squirrel dying on you, because this squirrel has got to be one of the most resilient mammals on the planet. And then this owl swoops down and grabs Allen the squirrel by the head and flies away."

Topher licks his finger before turning the next index card. "After Allen the squirrel was kidnapped, Allen the human would ask me, 'Where is your smile, my friend? Where is Topher Schmidt, my most positive and contagiously optimistic friend?' And I would say he died when Allen the squirrel was lifted above the treetops.' And Allen the human would say, 'It's not your fault.' And I would say 'I know,' but I was lying.

Topher pauses. His shoulders shrug a little as he brushes a tear from his eye. "I know this may sound silly, but seeing that little squirrel fly off really made me think about things. Like how short a time we have on this earth before life sinks its talons into our own heads and the lights go out for all of us for good."

Topher looks back down at his index cards. "I started teaching kindergarten a week after Allen the squirrel was murdered. For the next three weeks, it was all I could think about. I wasn't myself. I dressed in all black, and I started using my lesson plans to prepare the children for the bleak lives ahead of them.

"Then, two days ago, Allen the human paid me a visit. He knew I was in bad shape, so he took me out on a walk in the woods to get away from it all. For about an hour, I felt better. The smell of trees and the sounds of birds chirping was exactly what I needed.

"Then I heard an owl hooting up in a tree.

"'Just let it go, Topher,' Allen the human told me. 'Don't listen to him.' And he started holding me back as I approached the base of the tree. 'It's not worth it.'

"But I wasn't listening. 'Hey, owl!' I yelled. 'Yeah, I'm talking to you!' Then I started throwing rocks at the owl, but I kept missing.

"Allen the human was starting to get spooked we might get arrested by a park ranger, so he kept trying to pull me back up the trail.

"'No!' I screamed as I chucked rocks at the owl with one hand while I fought off Allen the human with the other. 'This is for Allen! This is for Allen!'"

Topher glanced up from his notes and looked curiously at his audience.

"But the owl didn't move. It just kept sitting there, taunting me with its hoots. So, I picked up a bigger rock. 'It's mocking me, Allen,' I said as I cocked my arm back.

"'Topher, chill!' Allen the human said. 'Didn't you notice it hasn't flown away?'

"'Yeah, because it's too full of squirrel!' I screamed back at him.

"'It's not even the same owl!' Allen said.

"'No owl is innocent,' I said, and I started to throw the rock.

"'Topher, no!' Allen yelled, and he blocked my arm, and the rock flew out sideways and hit the ground. Allen had a wild look in his eye. He still had a grip on my arm. 'I think the owl is injured,' he said, and he looked up.

"I looked up too. The owl was no more than twenty feet away, and I could see his left wing was a little crooked. But none of my rocks had hit it; the owl had been too hurt to move all along. 'No,' I said in disbelief, but I knew that he was right. The owl wasn't hanging out on the branch to mock me; he was doing it because he couldn't fly away.

"In that moment, this owl's pain and vulnerability and, yes, possibly even innocence—though I still haven't ruled out the possibility this owl was complicit in Allen the squirrel's murder—eclipsed my own anger, grief, and deep, deep primal desire for vengeance. I struggled to reconcile my cognitive dissonance: owls are evil, especially when they're flying away with your pet squirrel, but a wounded owl stuck in a tree? Well that was still a wounded animal, wasn't it? And didn't all wounded animals die the same miserable deaths? Cold, tired, and alone, until an apex predator came to eat them alive?

"So I started climbing the tree. I didn't care that Allen the human was yelling at me that I was going to fall to my death. And I didn't care how difficult it was to climb a tree in combat boots and skinny jeans. It didn't matter how much sap was sticking to my fingers, or how badly I was getting cut by razor-sharp pine needles. I was ascending into a higher state of consciousness.

"At the peak, I could see for miles. In the middle of a vast landscape of trees and snow-capped mountains, here I was: a mere ape clinging to the top of a douglas fir. And next to me: an injured owl, gasping what barely amounted to a hoot of surrender.

"Allen the human didn't scold me when I came back to earth with the owl cradled in my arm. He didn't say much as he drove me home. In fact, we didn't have a real conversation of substance until we were back in my house, tucking the owl into a makeshift bed in a shoebox after we'd mended its wing.

"'You know,' Allen said, 'taking care of an owl is a huge responsibility.'

"'I know,' I said.

"'You may wake up one day and want to throw it out the window,' he said.

"'No,' I said. 'I won't.'

"'Are you sure?' he said. 'I mean, you threw like ten rocks at it.'

"'I know,' I said. 'But that was before I understood.'

"'Understood what?' he said.

"I looked up at him and said, 'Even though this owl and I are both hurt, and even though we've hurt other people, that doesn't mean we can't heal together.'"

***

One Month Later - Halloween

Ten minutes after the lunch bell rings, I realize I'm still wearing my squirrel mask. Before I can take it off, Charlotte walks into my classroom wearing her tree costume. Some leaves fall out of her hair as she glances at the empty desks. The room is covered with paper cut-outs of ghosts, black cats, and pumpkins.

"No Topher?" she says as she takes a seat across from me.

I shake my head. "He went to lunch with the kids."

She nods. Even through the thick bark on her face, I can see a distant look in her eyes. She snaps out of it and sits up a little straighter, resting her branches on the desk. "I saw your ad in the break room."

"Oh yeah?" I say.

"Yeah," she says. "The one for the race car bed?"

I look away.

"I didn't know you had kids," she says.

I look down at my bushy squirrel tail, which is jammed underneath my chair leg. "I don't," I say. "I've slept in it since I was six."

"Oh," she says. "With no modifications?"

"Very few," I say. "Anyway, I figured it was time for a real bed."

She nods. "I think my niece would love it."

"Oh yeah?" I say.

"Yeah," she says. And then we sit there, just a squirrel and a tree enjoying a long, comfortable silence.

Mrs. Grieves opens the door and leans in. She's dressed as a mushroom. "It's time," she says.

Charlotte and I both nod and stand up. We follow Mrs. Grieves into the hallway, and then out the back door, to the path that leads to the playground. During a normal lunch hour, this playground would be packed with children running around, climbing the monkey bars, and going down the slide. But today, it's completely empty.

We reach the end of the playground, where a crowd of kindergarteners dressed as little princesses, super heroes, and cartoon characters have gathered in a clearing at the edge of the forest. They are all huddled in a semi-circle around Topher, who is dressed as an owl. Allen the human is sitting cross-legged next to him. Like me, he's dressed as a squirrel.

"There they are," Topher says, and all the children start giggling as they make a path for us to get closer. We kneel next to Topher, and look down at his wings crossed underneath his chest. Cradled in his feathery forearms is an owl dressed up as a mushroom spore. "Can you take Owl-len out of his costume?" Topher says. "I can't use my fingers."

Charlotte looks at me as she lifts her branches.

"I guess I can," I say, and I use my furry paws to unzip Owl-len from his sponge-like outfit. He flaps his wings and gently clasps his talons around Topher's wrist.

Topher starts to tear up. "I never thought this day would come."

Allen the human puts a squirrel claw on Topher's shoulder. "It's time," he says.

Topher nods and starts to lift his wing. But before Owl-len can fly away, we hear a voice calling out in the distance, "Not yet!" the voice says. We all turn to see Mrs. Barrett running up the hill. She remembered to wear her squirrel poop costume. "Wait!" she calls out. "Don't let him fly away!" Her words are not slurred. And even though her baggy brown costume flops side to side, she runs toward us in a perfectly straight line.

She reaches us just as Owl-len takes off. Everyone gasps as the bird rises higher, ascending toward the tops of the trees. Owl-len hoots as he flies over the forest, disappearing into the darkness of the woods.

I feel a tree branch hold my paw. I look down at it, and then up at Charlotte smiling at me through the small mouth hole in her bark mask. I want to smile back, but all I can think about is how dangerous and scary it is for an owl out in those woods. I can't help but imagine an eagle or a hawk swooping down and eating Owl-len, and I start to wonder if it would have been better if Owl-len had just stayed here, dressed up as a spore, living at Topher's house, and sleeping in the baby crib Topher purchased for him.

As if reading my mind, Charlotte leans toward me and whispers in my ear, "He's an owl again."

Topher catches my eye. Tears are streaming down his beak. He wipes them off with his wing as Allen pats his feathery back with a sympathetic squirrel claw.

"He sure is," I say. "He sure is."

THE HERO

The song is by Good Charlotte. Joey is sure of that much, even if he can't remember the name. It's the one about not giving into the system. And refusing to succumb to orthodox life choices. And maintaining a steadfast opposition to the nine-to-five fate that ends up being an almost inevitable consequence of living in a modern capitalist economy with an efficient division of labor. It's the one about having a kind of vague but earnest skepticism of society in general.

You know, that Good Charlotte song. Blasting out of a speaker on a public bus between North Hollywood and Downtown Los Angeles. The speaker is held by a man who looks like he could be in Good Charlotte—black skinny jeans, black t-shirt, and pink spiky hair with bangs that hang over his eyebrows a la Sia or maybe a sheepdog. He's not goth, per se. More of an emo, an endangered species of social strata that branched off from the goth phylum sometime in the late 1980s.

Joey stares at Good Charlotte. Good Charlotte smirks at the window. Good Charlotte knows Joey is staring at him, and his refusal to acknowledge Joey places them in the midst of a staring contest of sorts, with the vectors of their respective looks forming a right angle of unrequited attention.

The song ends. A new song begins. This one is also by Good Charlotte. A man next to Joey looks like he's considering using one of the bus's rubber handholds to hang himself.

The forty-six passengers of the southbound 162 line are, collectively, a large-diameter slice of America, a college brochure picture of diversity consisting of fourteen different ethnicities, eight religions, one PhD, four employees of the month, three people fired for bringing up controversial conspiracy theories at the office picnic, a nationally competitive clarinetist, two people who cut their sandwiches into triangles, four people who refuse to become organ donors for fear of some future apocalyptic scenario involving cloning, and a person who routinely kicks his dropped blueberries under the fridge in the office break room.

On account of the broken air conditioner, the bus is about twenty to thirty degrees hotter than usual. Sweat accumulates at the ends of noses. Air is less breathed than swallowed. Window-seated passengers are steaming.

The Furnace On Wheels groans to a stop and emits a complex sequence of mechanical hissing and whirring noises. More people board the bus. They appear hesitant to scan their Tap cards. When they woke up this morning, they probably hadn't planned on attending an emo concert in a greenhouse. But here they are. The doors close behind them before they can escape. This concert is standing-room only.

Joey loses the staring contest with Good Charlotte. He opts to glance around the bus with a look that says, This guy, right? This is something we will all silently disapprove of, together. An elderly Black man is rolling his eyes at Good Charlotte. A middle-aged white woman, seated near the back, is wearing a long toad-like frown. The young Hispanic guy with dueling sleeves of bible verses tattooed up his arms has reflexively given the roof's emergency exit a few wistful glances. Joey feels like Bible Tats is either the most- or least-likely person available to try to reason with Good Charlotte, but Bible Tats puts on his headphones and sits down.

When Bible Tats sits, Joey is able to look across the bus unobstructed for the first time. He catches sight of a college girl in a Wolfsuka t-shirt, a sight which, to Joey, seems impossible. He has never been able to find a fellow fan of the band in real life, and yet, on a bus somewhere north of downtown Los Angeles, here she is.

Joey feels a little paradise inside. He can see a Swiss chalet near a ski resort. The neighbors are friendly. They all throw parties and show off their chalets. Joey and the girl in the back of the bus have a chalet with high ceilings and a big fireplace with a limestone hearth and a mantle with a Native American hachette. Visitors to their chalet sometimes say, 'Hmm, a Native American hachette, huh?' And Joey says, 'Yeah.' And the visitors say, 'A little problematic, don't you think?' And Joey says, no, it was a gift from Wynemah, and she's a member of the Miwok tribe, and they, or at least she, granted Joey honorary membership, and Joey thinks it's a fairly reasonable assumption that the perks of this membership must include hanging the hachette above his mantle, since it was a gift after all. It is usually around this point that Joey directs his guests' attention to the Christmas card on the mantle, where Joey, the girl from the back of the bus, and their Alaskan Malamute, Balto, all wear matching green cardigans.

Good Charlotte is turning up his music. He has to very briefly look down at his speaker to find the volume buttons, but he makes sure to keep his head in a perfectly vertical track so that it doesn't make even the slightest lateral rotation which might cause him to inadvertently make eye contact with any of the other passengers who, by this point, are all fantasizing about slowly driving the bus back and forth over his spiky dyed head. When the volume has reached maximum capacity explosiveness-wise, he stops pushing the buttons to lift his head in the same vertical track as before. He continues smirking out the window.

Joey steals another glance at the girl in the back of the bus. She has a book in her hand—Dostoevsky. But she's too busy scowling at Good Charlotte to read. She makes another attempt at a page, sighs, slaps the book against her thigh, and resumes scowling. She catches Joey looking at her, and smiles at him, which causes Joey's heart to twist around in highly advanced yoga poses. She nods toward Good Charlotte and rolls her eyes. Joey lets out a very small nervous honking laugh that startles a young Hispanic mother with two children on her lap.

Joey looks at his work boots. He curses himself for getting his hopes up. He curses the daydream of the chalet, and then he curses all chalets. He curses the Swiss. He curses himself for thinking that a girl like that could ever love a guy like him. He wants to do something impressive, wants to reach out and backhand Good Charlotte upside the head. He's so close, so damn close, Joey knows he could do it if he wanted to. He'd just have to lean over this little Asian grandma, extend his hand and whack! He'd be a hero. He's never been a hero before—never even dreamt of the idea.

But he's not a hero. He's pretty sure heroes don't live with their alcoholic mothers and stepfathers in one-bedroom apartments above convenience stores. And heroes don't work less-than-minimum wage construction jobs off the books. And if a hero were to work such a job, and his boss—Barry, a leatherfaced construction pimp without an ounce of love for any one of his twenty-six desperately poor construction hoes—were to refuse to pay the hero everything he was due for a job, surely the hero would stand up for himself instead of nodding and walking away without a word?

The elderly Black man is asking Good Charlotte to please turn down the music, son, please for the love of god, we're all held captive here. Good Charlotte is as still as a tin man on the street. The girl in the back of the bus is tapping the side of her head against the window.

Joey is still considering the backhand. Firm, but not cruel. More of a message, a warning shot. The motivation is there for Joey. Good Charlotte has morphed into a composite of every construction pimp who ever wronged Joey, every school bully who tapped him in the nuts in the hallway, and every one of his mother's ex-boyfriends, even the ones who played catch with him, because catch with someone who doesn't remember your name gets old pretty quickly.

The girl in the back of the bus tucks her book in her bag and presses the Request Stop button. There isn't much time now. Any minute, the bus driver will exit under one of the pale green billboards hanging over the road, pull up to a curb, and open the doors for the girl to exit forever, forever thinking of Joey as that coward who let a guy with bangs hold fifty-three people prisoner on the southbound 162. In the cosmic battle between good and evil, Joey knows he must take a stand. The chalet is at stake.

So Joey grabs Good Charlotte's speaker and throws it out an open window.

Last Monday, at the start of a job building a gas station, Barry sent Joey to fetch him a carton of Senecas, and promised to pay Joey back. However, when Joey returned, Barry not only refused to reimburse him, but had also replaced Joey on the jobsite with someone else. A day after the speaker throwing incident, Joey would swear the handheld speaker looked just like a carton of Senecas on its way out the window.

Good Charlotte is slowly turning his head to the right. The bus is almost completely silent, the angsty noises from the speaker having faded into the distance almost instantaneously post-throw. Good Charlotte's eyes stop panning when they meet Joey's. Good Charlotte looks at him with respect. There's some loathing in there too. Astonishment made a brief appearance, but it was snuffed out pretty quickly. Joey, on the other hand, cannot hide his shock. None of what he just did had been conscious. His first instinct is to apologize, but he doesn't. Good Charlotte and Joey stare at each other. The bus rumbles to a stop.

The doors open. Good Charlotte loses the final staring contest. He hops off the bus and runs down the street. Joey waits for someone to say, 'Bravo,' or 'Well done,' or 'Thanks for doing that,' but everyone is looking at him with a mix of surprise and fear. The elderly Black man shakes his head as if to say, 'Bit of an overreaction.' The middle aged white woman has a look that says, 'I mean, yes, of course we were all annoyed, but what if you had caused a car accident?' Bible Tats has walked to the opposite end of the bus. The Hispanic mother is looking at Joey as if she's afraid he might, at any second, throw one of her kids out the window. The girl from the back of the bus is now the girl paused halfway out the door. She is the only one smiling at Joey. Joey's heart twists into another yoga pose—an impossible sleeping crane with pretzeled pulmonary veins above a couple aortae playing the roles of hands in a handstand. The girl paused in the doorway starts a slow clap. After five claps, no one has joined her. She steps off the bus. The doors close. The bus pulls away from the curb. Joey resolves to avoid eye contact with everyone around him; he has received all the praise he needs.

At the next stop, a man of very imposing stature boards the bus. He is bulging out of his leather jacket. He has a bruise above his right eye. And he is angry. He is screaming. He wants to know who threw a speaker into his open convertible and hit him in the face. Every single pair of eyeballs turns in Joey's direction. There is nowhere to hide.

Joey swims through the crowd to the back door. The imposing man is in hot pursuit. Joey jumps off the yellow painted step and lands prone on the curb. He clamors into a standing position and stumbles his way into a steady sprint. The imposing man chases Joey past a red convertible, and then a woman walking her dog, and then a house on the corner. The man is yelling at Joey, but Joey is faster than this guy. Within a minute, Joey is blocks ahead of his pursuer. The fog of adrenaline is lifting. Joey's cerebellum is rebooting. Joey doesn't know where he's running to, but he knows he needs to keep running—at least a little longer—to put a safe distance between him and the imposing man. And yet, if he runs too far, he might run into Good Charlotte. And then what? Apologize? For now, he will keep running, because as crazy as it sounds, there's still a chance he might find the girl from the back of the bus. And even though it's a slim chance, considering how much time has passed since he last saw her, it's worth it. For the first time in a long time, Joey feels like he's in control.

THE PUDGY BOY

Twenty-four years of life have blessed me with the wisdom that vanity is more of a science than an art.

Six sets of chest. Four sets of shoulders. Superset bis and abs. Never wear the same clothes twice. Only brush the front side of your teeth. And, most importantly, surgically alter your chin to get a perfectly symmetrical face.

That's what I did. And I must be doing something right, because I've had people come up to me at the gym, see my little 24 Hour Fitness badge, and say "Train me."

That happened twice. The rest of my clients have been a little harder to catch. It's fine. I'm only working here as a stepping stone. One day, I'll save up enough money to open my own gym across the street from 24. And when I do, I'm going to watch everyone flock to Blaine's Fitness.

In the meantime, I'm driving to clothing stores and putting my business card in the pocket of every pair of pants over a thirty-eight-inch waist. I've already gotten four clients this way. And today, I got a call from someone who is either going to kill me or make me rich.

***

I need advice. So I go to my best friend, Katya. Katya is the most elite trainer at 24. Too elite, actually. She has two PhDs, and should probably be working as a university professor or as a trainer for a professional sports team. The only reason why she's working at 24 Hour Fitness is because she served ten years in a Russian prison for allegedly murdering her husband by locking him in a sauna. Personally, I think he barricaded himself inside.

So I stroll up casually to Katya, who's doing pull-ups with four plates tied to her waist.

"Kats," I say, real casual. "Have you ever had a client ask you to do something kind of weird?"

"All the time," Katya says. "Then I grab his balls to show who is in control."

"Well I can't do that," I say. "This guy called me on the phone."

"What he say?"

I swallow and look across the gym at my crush, Sammy, as she leads a hip hop dance class. She is definitely out of earshot. "He, uh, said he wants me to come over to his house wearing nothing but a diaper and a bonnet. Then he wants me to sit in a high chair at his dining-room table and eat a large meal full of rich and fatty foods. And while I do that, he wants to say things like, 'Oh you're a pudgy boy aren't you?' And he said he'll give me a thousand dollars."

"Per session?"

I think about it. "Yes, every time I come over."

"How often?"

"Whenever I want."

Kayta squints as she continues doing pull-ups. "And he doesn't want…"

"No, no, no," I say, "this is strictly platonic."

She lets go of the bar and unties the plates around her waist. They hit the ground with a thud and clang against each other. "I think you should do it."

"Really?"

"I don't know how you can afford to wear different clothes every day."

I am over $20,000 in debt.

"Plus," she says, "you want to open gym." Katya puts more chalk on her hands and claps them together. "Dreams are expensive."

I look back at Sammy. She's got her class of middle-aged divorcees doing The Whole Shack Shimmy at high speed. Goddamn that's a hot dance craze.

"I'll think about it," I say, and start walking off.

"Oh, Blaine?" Katya says.

"Yeah?"

She jumps and grabs the pull-up bar. "Don't get murdered."

***

The house, according to Zillow, is worth $45 million dollars. The security guard opens the gate as soon as he sees me in my diaper and bonnet. I park my Civic next to a line of Aston Martins, Jaguars, Lamborghinis, Maseratis, and Ferraris. The house and courtyard remind me of The Getty.

"Welcome!" Clyde, the owner, says as he walks out one of his house's many front doors. He's holding a wooden cane and wearing a Gucci bathrobe and boxer shorts. His gut sways as he takes one elephantine step after another. He's somewhere in the ballpark of four hundred to five hundred pounds. "You're in better shape than I thought," he says to me.

"Yeah, that's my job," I say, looking down at myself.

He points at me with his cane. "Are those eight abdominal muscles? My goodness. You must do a lot of sit-ups. I haven't done a sit-up in forty years!"

"I can train you," I say.

"Oh ho!" he laughs, covering his massive belly with both hands. "You wish. Come on in!"

He takes me inside, past a caged lion, a replica soundstage of the Seinfeld coffee shop, and a fully assembled T-rex skeleton. He takes me into a room the size of a basketball court and sits me down in a high chair in front of a hundred-foot-long table made out of a redwood trunk sliced in half. Every type of junk food imaginable covers the table: burgers, hot dogs, French fries, chicken nuggets, pastas, cakes, ice cream, and in the middle of the table: a chocolate fountain, a cheese fountain, and a ranch dressing fountain.

"Fletcher, can you get Blaine his bib?" Clyde says as he sets up a microphone stand near his seat at the opposite end of the table. He taps the mic as he sits down. "Fletcher? Calling Fletcher. Blaine needs a bib."

A sewing needle of a man comes out of the shadows and fastens a monkey and kitten patterned bib around my neck. The monkeys and kittens look up at me with taunting eyes as they jump through hoops.

"All right, before we get started…" Clyde says softly into the mic, "...to receive your thousand-dollar payment, you will need to consume at least ten-thousand calories in a single sitting. Fletcher will keep track of your calorie count, and I will sit here, saying whatever I want into my little microphone. Once you have hit your caloric requirements, you will be handed a thousand dollars in cash and returned to your car, unharmed. Agreed?"

I raise my hand.

"Yes, Blaine."

"You didn't mention anything about the minimum ten-thousand calories."

"If you don't like the agreement, you can step down from your high chair and walk away."

I look out at the table of food. I had purposefully eaten dinner beforehand so I wouldn't eat too much junk food tonight.

"That's okay, I'm cool with it," I say, and pick up a triple cheeseburger. I'm self-conscious when people watch me eat, so I take a small bite. Fletcher makes a note on his clipboard. A little grease dribbles down my chin as I chew.

Clyde leans in toward his microphone. "Oh you like that cheeseburger, don't you?"

***

Fletcher hands me the money in one-dollar bills stacked neatly in a paper grocery bag. He also hands me a wad of napkins and a 1099.

"Brilliant work," he says, and shuts one of the front doors.

On my drive home, I distract myself from my stomach pains by thinking about how I'm going to spend my new cash. Sure, I could pay down my debt, but Clyde said I could come by whenever I wanted. If I come every day, I can knock out my debt in less than a month. If I come more than once a day, I could be debt free in a little over a week.

Clearly, now is not the time to pay down debt. Now is the time to upgrade my life.

***

I get up at five am, clog the toilet, and hit the gym hard. If Michael Phelps eats twelve thousand calories a day, I simply have to train as hard as Michael Phelps. I swim for two hours, run for an hour, toss absurd amounts of weight around for an hour, and then run for another hour. It's hard to train my clients in between workouts, not only because of my lack of time and energy, but also because I find my motivation dwindling. Thirty bucks a client is starting to sound pretty weak when I know I have a thousand dollars within reach whenever I want it.

I decide to tell Katya about my dilemma while we ride exercise bikes.

"You can't quit," she tells me.

"I'm making more money than I've ever made in my life," I say, panting as I pedal harder. "I don't need to slave away teaching Pilates to grandmas. I can start my own gym."

"Not yet," she says. She picks up forty pound dumbbells off the floor and curls them as she pedals. "You need money. And you need to work out. You already look fat."

Her words slice through me like a vegetable knife to the kidney.

"I'm just a little bloated, okay?" I say. I lift up my shirt to show her my eight pack. The sight of my eight perfect cubes glistening in the mirror comforts me.

"You are soft on the inside," Katya says, and starts doing shoulder raises as she pedals.

I catch sight of Sammy passing by in the hall.

"Maybe I will stick around after all," I say. I hop off my bike and make my way to the door. "Watch this."

***

Out in the hallway, I look over my shoulder. I see Katya peeking around the cycling room door. I wink at her and walk up next to Sammy.

"If our Lord wasn't testing us," I say in a booming voice, "how would you account for the proliferation, these days, of this obscene rock and roll music?"

Sammy stops to stare at me.

"Footloose," I say. "John Lithgow. Kevin Bacon."

"What?" Sammy says.

"It's an 80s movie. A small-town preacher tries to make rock and roll and dancing illegal. Ring a bell?"

Sammy blinks.

"You haven't seen it?" I say. "I can't believe someone who teaches dance classes hasn't seen Footloose!"

"I'm sorry. What's your name again?"

"Blaine," I tell her.

"Right, Blaine."

"I'm a trainer here."

"Of course you are. I'm sorry, Blaine. What were you saying?"

"Nothing." I put my hand in my pocket and pull out a folded up piece of printer paper. "So, this is totally crazy, but I bought a couple of front row seats for The Ad Guys, the world's hottest new boy band. My buddy flaked on me, so now I have an extra ticket. Would you want to go?"

I hand her the paper. She scrutinizes it, bewildered.

Booyah.

"Aren't these like hundreds of dollars?" she says.

"A thousand," I say. "Well, eleven-hundred twenty-six after taxes and fees."

She hands the paper back to me. "I'm sorry, but I'm making dinner with my roommate tonight. Sounds super fun, though!" She smiles and waves as she walks away.

After she turns the corner, I toss the tickets in the trash.

A thousand dollars means nothing to me now.

***

Jalapeno poppers are on the menu tonight. I wash them down with a blueberry milkshake.

"How's that ice cold milkshake?" Clyde says.

"Sweet," I say.

"Is it tasty?"

I nod as I scoop whipped cream onto a cheesecake. "What's my calorie count?" I say to Fletcher.

Fletcher consults his clipboard. "Five thousand four hundred and…" He takes his pencil out from behind his ear and makes a note. "...seventy eight."

"You want some pizza?" Clyde says, pointing with his cane. "You're going to want to swim around in this cheese."

I tell Fletcher to fetch me some pizza. "And dip it in the ranch fountain while you're at it," I tell him.

"Oooooh," Clyde says. "You won't put it through the cheese fountain too."

"I'll be damned if I don't," I say. "Drag it through the cheese fountain," I bark at Fletcher.

"Yes, sire," Fletcher says. He returns with two tongs full of dripping pizza.

"That's gonna get messy," Clyde coos.

I tip my head back and open my mouth like I'm at the dentist. "Just shovel it in," I say.

***

Five am.

Bathroom. Bike. Swim. Run. Swim. Weights. Pilates.

"You're breaking out," Katya tells me while we stretch.

I see Sammy coming out of her dance class. Cardi B blasts from the speaker.

"I don't care," I say, and jog over to Sammy.

"Jonas Brothers tickets!" I say.

"Wow, you really love boy bands," she says as we walk down the hall.

I flip open the folded up printer paper. "Only when I get front row seats."

"Wow, front row seats again," she says, taking the tickets to examine them. She hands them back to me. "Say, Blaine, if you don't mind me asking, where are you getting two thousand dollars to throw at front row seats two nights in a row?"

I freeze. "What?"

She straightens her headband. "I'm sorry, that was really rude of me." She starts to leave. "I'm making dinner with my roommate again tonight," she says, "but have a super fun time!"

I can read between the lines. This woman loves to cook.

"Wait, Sammy!" I say. "I'm starting my own gym."

She cocks her head to the side.

"That's how I got the money."

She cautiously walks back to me. "Your own gym?"

"Yeah, I just use this place to get clients. Then I secretly train them after work so I don't have to split the pot with the gym. I make stacks."

I could see the first spark of intrigue appear in her eyes. "And you have your own space to train?"

I pause. "I just train them in their homes. But I'm saving up for a space." I pause again. "When I'm not buying Jonas Brothers tickets."

She nods, impressed.

"Listen," I say, "why don't I come over sometime? You and your roommate can cook me dinner. I can tell you all about my gym."

"No," she says. "But catch me tomorrow. Maybe we can meet somewhere for coffee?"

***

Bacon. A pound of rigatoni. Twelve croissants. A gallon of eggnog. Four chocolate chip pancakes. Two T-bone steaks. Eight fried cheese sticks.

"Ooooh you're a cheesy boy, aren't you?"

***

"I just really don't want a boss," Sammy tells me.

We're in a fancy coffee shop. I can afford it.

"And I don't want to keep giving so much of my money to a big corporation," she says. "I hate feeling like I'm owned."

The coffee is getting to me. I excuse myself to the restroom. When I return to the table a half-hour later, I'm fifteen pounds lighter. "You were saying."

"No, it's stupid," she says, and sips her latte.

"No, it's not. I'm going rogue. You can do it too."

"Well," she says, "actually, I'm thinking of doing something a little bit different from you. I'm thinking of starting a YouTube channel."

"That's great! You would be so good." A thought dawns on me. "We would be so good."

She grimaces. "Well…"

I stand and lift up my shirt to show her my abs.

"Blaine, sit your ass down."

I do.

"Never do that again," Sammy says, looking around.

"I'm sorry. I just think we would make a great team."

She frowns at me. Then looks down at my torso. Then back up at me. "Can you buy us a camera?"

***

A twenty-eight ounce bag of cheetos. Eight red velvet cupcakes. A serving bowl full of macaroni and cheese. Two tins of pringles. A box of Cheez-its. Three chicken sandwiches.

"Calorie count?"

"Eight thousand, six hundred and…fifty eight."

"Get me some of that deep fried butter."

"Yeah you like butter, don't you? You want to slide into a bathtub of butter and let it congeal."

***

"What's up, Fitness Freaks. It's Sammy."

"And I'm Blaine!"

"And we're here to…"

"Get! You! Fit!"

***

On the morning of the third week, I look in the mirror. It's worse than I thought.

I show Katya as soon as I get to the gym.

"A six-pack," she says, staring at my abs.

I lower my shirt.

"You're slipping, Blaine."

"I know," I say, rubbing my eyes. "But I can't take a day off. We needed a new camera for our YouTube channel. Then we needed a mic. Then editing software. Then Sammy wanted to lease a small studio in Beverly Hills."

"At least you have your gym."

"She has her gym. She has everythings she needs. I still need to drive back here to use the weights. And guess what? My car broke down. And I have bed bugs."

Sammy jogs up to us and continues running in place. "Hey," she says. She's sweating and has a little headset on. "I have to get to my next class, but after work, I'm teaching jazzercise in the studio. Fifty people signed up."

"That's great," I tell her. "Wow, fifty people."

"Yeah," she says, breathing hard. "But the capacity for the studio is forty-five. Would you mind leasing a bigger studio?"

Katya looks at me.

"Sure," I say.

"Great," Sammy says. "Do it this afternoon. I have to get the email out with the new address. Thanks!"

***

Halfway through a loaf of bread stuffed with chorizo, I pause. I set the bread down on the little tray attached to my high chair and squint across the table.

"That's some yummy bread," Clyde says. "Yummy yummy."

Clyde looks different, somehow. But I can't put my finger on it.

Then, Fletcher comes in from the kitchen with a salad and sets it in front of Clyde.

"Thank you, Fletcher," Clyde says. He daintily cuts a piece of spinach in half and nibbles on the end of it.

My eyes get wide. "You've lost weight."

"Forty pounds," he says. "It's amazing what you can accomplish with a little hard work."

"How did you make your money?"

"My father was an oil baron."

I nod and pick up my chorizo loaf.

I set it back down. "Clyde, if you don't mind me asking...why do you...you know…"

"Enjoy watching you stuff your face?"

My bonnet bobs forward as I nod.

Clyde grins and takes another bite of spinach. "Because it entertains me."

***

"Hey, Fitness Freaks, it's May!" I say to the camera. "And you know what that means!" I lift up my shirt. "Time to work on that summer bod!"

Sammy looks at me in horror. "Turn off the camera," she says, pulling my shirt down.

I do as I'm told.

"What the hell is this?" she says, pointing at my stomach.

I look at our freshly redone floor. "I'm sorry. I've just been so busy with the channel, I haven't been to the gym as much."

"But what are you eating?" she says, disgusted. "It looks like you've put on twenty pounds."

Thirty-six.

"I'll lose them."

"You need to do better than lose them. You need to lose them plus another ten. If we want to be the biggest fitness influencers on YouTube, we need to be fitter than the fittest. We need to be hyper fit."

"Yes, sire."

"What'd you say?"

"Nothing."

Sammy pulls out her phone and starts swiping pictures of a convention center, "By the way, we need tickets to the Life Goals Health and Wellness Expo. And if you could get some weights in this studio, that would be great. A lot of our regulars are asking for them."

I pinch the layer of fat building just below my belly button. "I'll see what I can do."

***

My food cravings are getting worse. I find myself eating chips and burgers even when I'm at home. At Clyde's house, the feast is no longer a chore; it's something I look forward to.

At the fitness convention, Sammy can barely look at me. She tells me to go exploring while she works the booth and gives the presentation on stage.

I appear less and less frequently in our videos. If I'm lucky, Sammy will dress me up in a chef's outfit and film me in the kitchen.

One day, I can't unlock the door to our studio. Sammy meets me outside.

"Oh my god," she says, "did you not check your email? You need to check your email, Blaine."

"What's in my email?"

She gives me the same look she gave me when she turned me down for the boy band concerts. "I'm sorry, Blaine. But have a super fun day!"

I tell Katya everything when I get to the gym. She rides a Peloton while I sit on an exercise ball.

"Forget her," Katya says. "Now you can open your own gym."

I shake my head. "It's too late, Katya."

"What do you mean it's too late? This is your dream, Blaine."

"Was, Katya. Was."

I turn in my letter of resignation to 24 Hour Fitness later that day.

***

By December, I've ballooned to nearly three-hundred pounds. Clyde, who used to be easy to spot from across the table, has shrunken down to a man half his size. Sometimes, he'll answer the door right after a workout, and he'll lift his shirt to wipe sweat off his forehead. His skin is loose and sagging, but I can see the outline of abs.

"You look different," he tells me. "Have you lost weight?" Then he leads me into his house. The caged lion watches me closely as I pass by.

It now takes Fletcher and six other assistants to lift me into my high chair, a new contraption that Clyde had reinforced with titanium bars. I salivate as I point at food with my thick fingers. Fletcher gives me Clyde's old cane so I can point without raising my arms. I don't ask for the calorie count anymore. I eat until it hurts.

After wolfing down an entire tin of brownies, I sit back to catch my breath.

"You've performed admirably, Blaine," Clyde says into his microphone. "I would like to reward you with a bonus."

I nod a few centimeters.

"I would like to give you my house."

***

I don't get out of bed much anymore. It requires too many assistants to roll me out. I will probably die in this bed, calling on Fletcher to fetch me more chicken wings until I gasp my last breath.

Clyde still comes over sometimes. He sits in the corner and whispers words of encouragement into his microphone. 'One more taco.' 'Finish the breadstick.' Things like that. He's built a really incredible fitness brand with Sammy. I think they might be engaged.

Katya used to call me, begging to train me, to whip me back into shape. I blocked her number.

This is who I am now.

This is who I always will be.

***

Ten years into my new life, Fletcher comes into my room with the mail and a tray full of muffins. I devour the muffins while I sort through my letters.

A large manila envelope catches my eye. It's addressed to 'The Current Pudgy Boy.' I tear it open.

Inside is a stack of photographs of four-hundred-pound men sitting across from super ripped dudes in baby outfits. A chill runs down my spine as I flip through the photos.

Flip

A four-hundred-pound man sits at the end of a table. A ripped man eats lasagna at the other end.

Flip.

The ripped man is now the fat man. He watches as a new ripped man wipes barbecue sauce from his chin.

Flip.

The barbecue sauce guy is now the fat man. He watches as a new ripped man eats rum cake with his hands.

The photos get grainier and grainier as I flip through them. The last five photos are black and white.

Flip.

A four-hundred-pound man in a three-piece suit and a top hat watches a guy munching on a turkey leg the size of my calf. And in the background:

Fletcher.

He's the same age.

I turn the photograph around. There's a date in the corner.

July 4th, 1921.

"No," I say aloud.

I keep flipping through the photos.

August 17th, 1911.

Fletcher is in the background.

January 28th, 1901.

Fletcher is in the background.

I keep flipping photos.

May 3rd, 1861.

Fletcher is spoon-feeding a very fit Union soldier in a baby outfit. The soldier's high chair is on the edge of a battlefield in the Civil War. A large general watches.

I flip to the next photo, which is actually a painting of an obese man in Italy in 10 A.D.

Fletcher is in the background wheeling in a wagon full of ham hocks for a Roman soldier in a diaper and a bonnet.

I grab the bullhorn off my nightstand and demand that Fletcher enter my living quarters immediately.

Fletcher leans around the door frame and peeks into my room. "Yes?" he says. He asks if he can bring me a bucket of bacon-wrapped scones or something.

I point at the photographs scattered around my comforter.

He nods knowingly. "It's time," he says. He leaves the room for a moment.

When he returns, he hands me a business card for a personal trainer.

Bryce Bigsby Fitness, it reads. *Your dream is my mission.*

I take out my phone and dial Bryce's number.

MY NAME IS JERRY

While I realize many people may disagree with me, especially those unlucky few who have had both their arms and legs eaten, I don't think anyone would deny that I have a certain amount of authority—an expertise, if you will—on the topic at hand, and therefore feel absolutely confident in my conviction that the worst thing about getting attacked by a shark is that everyone starts to see you as That Guy Who Got Attacked By A Shark.

May, 2011. I'm getting a beer at my old neighborhood bar with some friends from high school. Wayne. Karen. Faye. Pee Pants. I think we're going to reminisce about the good old times, like when Pee Pants nearly got hypothermia because he peed his pants on the chairlift and tried to ski down a double black diamond and knocked himself unconscious after a failed backflip off a mogul, but no, they want me to lift up my flannel shirt so they can all ogle at the waning moon shape of negative space where the shark bit off a chunk of my torso.

I let them ooh and aah for a couple minutes, but when they start to run their fingers down the jagged bite mark in my skin, I pull down my shirt and try to change the subject by asking Wayne about the Instagram post I saw of him riding an elephant in Thailand.

No one seems to hear me. Karen, who thinks she's some sort of animal behavior expert because she watched a lot of Discovery Channel after drinking her way out of a job as a ferris wheel operator, starts giving me advice about how I should have punched the shark or something.

And before I can tell her that I'll keep that in mind for my next shark attack, I hear Faye ask me this really pointed question like, "Well, were you provoking the shark?" And while I am tempted to remind this self-proclaimed animal rights activist of the time she left her cat home alone while she was at Burning Man, I hold my tongue. I take a deep breath. And I tell her no, I was just snorkeling, and she goes, "Hmmm," like that. "Hmmm." And then, as she lifts her beer to her lips, she mutters, "Well, imagine if someone tried to snorkel into your home."

So I point out that she didn't have anything critical to say about Wayne riding elephants in Thailand, but Faye just gives me this wide-eyed look of horror, not about the brutality of taming elephants, but rather because she thinks I'm suggesting Wayne might have hurt one of the elephant's backs by sitting on it. Granted, Wyane did just lose a bunch of weight, and he's a little sensitive about it.

"Are you okay?" Karen asks me. "You seem a little wound up."

"Of course he's okay," Pee Pants says. "You can't keep Shark Attack down for long."

"Ha!" Wayne says. "Ha! Yes!" And he points at me. "Shark Attack!"

"Shark Attack!" Karen says.

"Shark Attack!" Faye says.

And I smile and drink my beer and act like I'm totally cool with being the new Pee Pants, but the whole time, I'm thinking, My name is not Shark Attack. My name is Jerry.

***

A few days later, I'm opening a Tinder account, and I write a bio that goes something like:

My name is Jerry. I'm a grammy-award-winning saxophonist. I like hiking, saxophone, and brunch. You can catch me at the top of a mountain, playing saxophone and eating a poached egg.

The first couple messages aren't promising.

"Hypothetically, if we were to get married, and I wanted to take a cruise, would you feel comfortable getting on and off the ship if we made sure to blindfold you as you walked down the gangway?"

Or, "Let's say we get married and buy a home where the master bathroom is in the exact opposite corner of the house and three stories removed from the TV room. Would you be okay with me taking a bath while you watch TV—granted that we take all the necessary precautions you won't get triggered by the sound of sloshing water—or do you think the mere thought of a human submerged in liquid would send you into a flashback?"

Finally, I meet a girl who says, "I love saxophone!"

And I say, "Great. Your bio says you don't pay attention to the news."

"Nope."

"And you don't have social media?"

"Nope."

"Ever read a tweet?"

"I don't know what that is."

"And you love saxophone?"

"Love it."

Her name is Wendy.

So I invite Wendy to a Dodgers game and we get garlic fries and do the wave and drink margaritas and yell at Cardinals fans and don't talk at all about how I got six of my ribs pulled out of my flesh by a twenty-five-foot-long great white shark in Hanalei Bay.

It is easily the best date I have had since the shark attack. Then, in the seventh inning, it all goes south.

We sit down after singing Take Me Out To The Ball Game, and I put my arm around her and she snuggles up next to me, and just as I'm leaning in to ask if she wants to go with me to this falafel festival in Venice Beach on Thursday, this guy comes on the loudspeaker and asks everyone to stand if they are a veteran. And some people stand, and we start clapping, and eventually they sit down, and the clapping ends, and I lean toward Wendy to ask her about the falafel festival when the guy comes back on the loudspeaker and says, "Ladies and Gentlemen, if you have been attacked by a shark, please stand so we can honor you."

So I sit back and sip my beer and act like everyone else, looking around to see if anyone is standing. And no one is standing up, so the guy on the loudspeaker goes, "Hmm, are we sure no one here has been attacked by a shark?"

And I'm shoveling garlic fries in my mouth at this point, shaking my head, not trying to make a big scene or anything, but internally feeling a little frustrated by this guy's persistence, and silently hoping he'll shut his mouth and get back on the organ.

But he doesn't. He goes, "Really? No one has suffered any injuries at the mouth of an aquatic animal? No one has had any bones crushed in the jaws of a macropredatory beast? No one at this baseball game has ever been mauled by a prehistoric killing machine?"

"Nope," I say out loud. I'm looking over the railing, waiting for the game to get going again, but all the players are looking up into the stands from the dugout, waiting for someone to stand up so we can all honor them.

And Wendy crosses her arms and purses her lips and says, "I just don't understand why anyone would swim in the ocean. We have so many bodies of water reserved just for humans: pools, public pools, man-made lakes." She turns to me. "Did you know that Scandinavians don't swim in the ocean in Scandinavia? Why can't Americans be more like the Scandinavians? Hmmm?"

And I stand up and start shuffling down the aisle while everyone in Dodger stadium cheers and applauds for me.

Wendy chases after me, but I've become quite fast since having six of my ribs, a kidney, and an eighth of my liver torn out of my oblique area with eighteen thousand Newtons of bite force, and I manage to drive out of the parking lot before she can catch up.

Over the next week, I do a lot of musician-grade heroin. I don't pick up my phone. When I finally check my voicemail, I listen to messages like:

"Shark Attack, it's Faye. Pee Pants is dead. Call me back."

Or "Jerry, it's your agent. I know you've never been a fan of getting attacked by sharks, but I think you owe it to all the shark attack victims out there to start making music about getting attacked by sharks. All right? Listen to me, Jer. Imagine a child: young, innocent, impressionable, recovering in the hospital after a savage great white attack, watching music videos on YouTube, and he doesn't see a single saxophonist that has been attacked by a shark. All his favorite artists like Lil Xan and—I don't know who the youths are listening to these days—but the point is that all the musicians have intact limbs and heads and torsos and not a single bite mark. Don't you think you owe it to that kid to get back up on stage? Yes? No? Call me."

Or "Shark Attack, it's Faye again. Where the hell are you? Pee Pants' funeral is tomorrow. Call me back."

Or "Hey, Jerry, it's Wendy. Give me a call when you get a chance."

Or "Are you kidding me, Shark Attack? We buried Pee Pants without you."

So I pack my bags—figuratively speaking. I don't actually have to pack any bags, because I'm flying to Hawaii, and when you're planning on committing suicide by shark attack, you don't have to pack anything; you can just wear your swim trunks on the plane. But it's kind of cold in LA on the day I'm supposed to leave, so I wear my swim trunks under my jeans, kind of like when I forget to do laundry, run out of boxers, and have to wear swim trunks, but that's besides the point. The point is that I'm going back to Hawaii, and this time, I'm not coming back.

On the way to the airport, I decide to stop by Pee Pants' grave.

It turns out he's buried in this kind of dumpy cemetery with brown grass and dead leaves everywhere, but I tough it out, and hike over to his plot, and kneel down next to it and set down a bouquet of flowers, and read his headstone, which says something like, "Steve 'Pee Pants' something. Nineteen-eighty-something to last week."

And just as I get up to leave, I hear this voice behind me say, "Doesn't really matter what they put on your headstone, does it?" And I turn around and realize it's Pee Pants' mom.

"I'm so sorry about Pee Pants," I say.

And she grits her teeth and balls her hands into fists and says, "His name is Steve."

And then we hug and get coffee and catch up, and I tell her all about the hellhole I've been in ever since I got attacked by a shark, and she lowers her head and looks kind of sad and I think she's going to tell me how sorry she feels for me, but instead she grabs my arm and gives it a little shake and says, "I'm just so glad you're all right."

And I laugh and say, "Yeah, yep, uh huh."

And she goes, "No, really. Do you know how many times this week I've had to explain what heli-skiing is?" And she kind of studies my face and the way I'm slowly nodding at her and she says, "Really? You haven't heard of it? It's when you jump out of a helicopter and ski down the mountain. At least, you're supposed to ski down the mountain."

And I say, "Right, right."

And she sighs and says, "Just be happy you aren't remembered for something like that."

And I ask her if she was listening to anything I just told her. I'm That Guy Who Got Attacked By A Shark, remember?

And she says, "You're still kicking aren't you? You're still breathing air. Your heart is still beating. That shark hasn't dragged you down to the bottom of the ocean yet, has it?"

And I say, "No."

And she says, "That's the spirit," and takes out an urn and hands it to me.

"What's this?" I say as I take it.

She shrugs. "Steve's father wanted to bury Steve. I wanted to cremate him. So we split him."

So I drive to Wendy's house and knock on her door, and when she opens it, I kiss her like I've never kissed anyone in my life. I tell her I want to swim in the ocean again. And she looks a little sad and says this isn't going to work out.

So I catch my flight to Hawaii, and this little old lady sitting next to me on the plane asks me what I'm going to do in Oahu, and I hold up an urn and tell her I'm spreading the ashes of the upper half of my friend Steve's body in the ocean. And she asks me who Steve was, and I tell her he was this really great skier who loved remote backcountry terrain, old Mustangs, making crop circles, golden retrievers, and Wayne's sister. I also tell her he was chopped in half by a helicopter propeller.

And she says, "That's nice," but it's okay because I'm pretty sure she tuned out before she heard that last part.

And then she tells me she has a granddaughter who is about my age.

"Has she ever heard of a grammy-award-winning saxophonist named Jerry Wiles?" I ask her.

The old lady kind of squints at me and says, "Jerry who?"

And I say, "What about swimming in the ocean? How does she feel about that?"

And the little old lady says she isn't too sure of her granddaughter's opinion of ocean swimming.

So I ask her if she's aware of her granddaughter holding any strong prejudices against people who get attacked by sharks, and the little old lady says she isn't aware of any such prejudices in her granddaughter.

So I sit back and kind of smile, and the little old lady writes down her granddaughter's number on a paper napkin and gives it to me. And I fold up the napkin and put it in my pocket even though I have absolutely no intention of texting some random old lady's granddaughter. And then I hold the urn full of Steve's ashes a little tighter to my chest, and look out the window at an ocean full of eight-hundred pound beasts that want to eat me alive, and I think to myself, "Not today. Not today."

***

The guy sitting next to me at the bar lifts his chin off his hand, revealing a knuckled imprint on his jawline. He blinks a couple times. "That was a story," he says as he turns his attention to his beer, which is still full. I'm killing the last of mine when he squints at me and says, "So you're telling me that Steve's mom buried only his legs?"

And I tell him, "No, Steve's dad buried his legs. Steve's mom burned Steve's top half."

The guy nods and hunches back over his beer. I'm starting to think I might have wasted my story on this guy when he says, "You know, I'd already heard of you. Before you told me all this."

And I go, "Yeah?"

And he says, "Yeah. I wasn't a big saxophone guy until I heard Sidestroke to Shore." He chuckles and shakes his head. "You lit up the world on that one, Jerry."

The compliment is bittersweet. "Actually, I wrote that after I got attacked by—"

"By a shark. I know that now," he says, and puts a hand on my shoulder. His wrist is covered in tattoos. "But I didn't know that when I listened to it. All I knew was that you were in pain." He slaps some folded up bills on the bar and stands up. While he puts on his jacket he says, "That whole record got me through prison." Then he pats me on the shoulder and walks out of the bar.

I sit in silence for a half hour before I pay my tab and leave. It takes me another half hour to swing by my house to pick up my saxophone on the way to the cemetery. The full moon makes it easy to find Steve's grave. And even though it's a chilly night, I don't hesitate to rip my shirt off and toss it into the wind.

I put my sax in my mouth and start playing Sidestroke to Shore with a passion I haven't felt since I penned it, and right when I get to the chorus, I arch my back and belt the notes at the stars, letting the moonlight shine through the jagged emptiness in my side and land on the grave of Steve's legs.

THE
MASTER
CONVERSATIONALIST

The Master Conversationalist went to the party because nothing gave him quite the same pleasure as absolutely dominating people in the arena of conversational combat. It was the same reason he went to any social event. A dodge here, a parry there, get wrist control, and then thrust the dagger under the ribs of an interlocutor with an obscure Latin phrase. That was how The Master Conversationalist did things. *Ab abusu ad usum non valet consequentia.*

Also, Greg had a wine cellar, which was the other reason why The Master Conversationalist went to the party.

So, now, with a glass of Greg's wine in his hand, The Master Conversationalist sauntered across the drawing room to a circle of people chatting outside the parlor. The circle was a carousel of familiar faces from the country club—Barbara, Clifford, Margot, Douglas—but The Master Conversationalist knew it would take a lot more than speaking their affluent dialect to divide et conquer the citizens of this little chat.

Context was critical. Hijacking a conversation halfway through was a bit like stealing a moving car—you've got some catching up to do, and even if you do get your hands on the wheel, you better kick the driver completely out of the vehicle if you want to turn that baby around. And who should so happen to be in the driver's seat at this very moment? That's right. The Master's nemesis, Ada Cratchett.

At the moment, Cratchett was talking about films, but he could tell by the way her pupils dilated a little at the sight of him that she was thinking something like"You again" or "Dare you challenge my authority on film criticism?" or simply *"Caelum non animum mutant qui trans mare currunt."*

But just as The Master Conversationalist prepared to punt Ada Cratchett out of the conversational Buick, Cratchett brought the discussion to a halt.

"Hello, Frank," she said, once again 'forgetting' that The Master

Conversationalist went by Francois now.

"Hello, Ada," The Master said.

"Did you read my latest review?" she said. A dimple appeared on her cheek. All heads in the chat swiveled to see The Master's reaction.

The Master gave his wine glass a quarter-turn. Oh, Ada. Still reviewing films like the twentieth-century journalist she was. It was time to checkmate this dinosaur. "I haven't," he said casually, glancing at his manicured fingernails, "I've been a little too busy reviewing the reviews of art films."

"Ah," Ada said. "Reviews of reviews?"

The Master looked bored as he swirled Greg's wine. "Indeed."

"So meta," Ada said.

"Well, it's more para-meta," The Master said, "but sure."

"Para-meta."

"Yes."

"Interesting," Ada said. "I think it's more trans-meta. Kind of like your review of A.O. Scott's review of Remorse Considered." She let out a little laugh before raising her wine glass to her lips, "But you already knew I felt that way."

The Master's right eyelid began to twitch. "You read my review of A.O. Scott's review of Remorse Considered?"

Ada cackled. "Oh, I didn't just read it darling. I reviewed it in *The Heron*."

The Master felt one of his testicles lift up into his body. "*The Heron*?"

"*The Heron*. I just published it thirty-six minutes ago."

The Master swallowed. Her move was brilliant. Lure The Master Conversationalist into a chat while she had an audience, then humiliate him by making him appear out-of-the-know. He hadn't been this embarrassed since the Café Gentrifique open-mic poetry slam when he soiled his trousers.

"I don't think I've read it yet," he said quietly.

Ada clucked her tongue. "I'm surprised, Frank," she said. "You're usually so well-read."

***

Cratchett's Critiques #100: Ada Cratchett Reviews Frank Petit's Review of A.O. Scott's review of Remorse Considered

If someone were inclined to write a negative review of A.O. Scott's review of Remorse Considered*—a ten-second-long silent film made by a schizophrenic Austrian filmmaker in 1899 about a cat batting around a ball of yarn—I would hope the critic didn't have a* *citrus allergy, because there are several pieces of fruit hanging so incredibly low, it's nearly impossible not to run into one. But Frank Petít somehow missed all of them.*

How?

Because he was too busy ranting about how A.O. Scott failed to proffer an adequate exposé on the yarn industry of nineteenth-century Europe.

Why, you might ask, would he go off on such a rant?

For the same reason he rambled about Danish watercolor paintings in his review of David Denby's review of Casablanca; it's why he blathered on about the history of the Irish Republican Army in his review of Caryn James' review of Die Hard; and it's why, in his own review of Citizen Kane, he waxed ad nauseum about the history of sledding:

Because Frank Petít is That Guy.

You know, That Guy at the party who holds people in a conversational prison from which they can't escape.

On the surface, his knowledge is impressive, but if you think for a moment, you'll realize any guy can appear this knowledgeable if he has the gall to insist that everyone follows a conversational compass of his own design, a compass that always points back to the subjects he reads about on Wikipedia.

In this way, having a conversation with Frank Petít is a bit like searching for something on Google, and then clicking on the twenty-fifth page of search results; what you read is going to be only tangentially related to what you searched for.

Believe me, I know. I talk to Frank Petít all the time.

Are you planning on telling Frank Petít about your honeymoon in Barcelona? Be prepared for a fifteen-minute analysis of The Persistence of Memory. Did you just tell Frank Petít you're an architect? Brace yourself. The Ludwig Mies van der Rohe lecture is coming. And don't even try to talk to this guy about blockchain or keto.

Should it surprise any of us that the man who cannot hold a normal conversation in real life is equally inept at writing a normal review of a review?

So, in honor of Frank's tangents, allow me a tangent of my own.

A few days ago, my niece, Cleo, told me about a boy in her kindergarten class who will not play catch with her at recess. The boy will pretend he wants to play, but when Cleo throws the ball to him, he promptly chucks it into the woods. Cleo will retrieve the ball and throw it back to him, at which point the boy will once again chuck the ball into the woods. This goes on for a while: Cleo throwing the ball, the boy throwing the ball into the woods, Cleo going to get the ball, and so on.

So Cleo asks me what to do about this boy. She wants to play catch, but the boy seems to want to play a very different game.

A very different game indeed.

I explained to Cleo that the boy doesn't want to play catch with her at all. No, he just wants to be an asshole.

So there you have it, readers. I think we have all learned a valuable lesson today. Give your time to someone who's willing to play catch. Not someone who hogs the ball. Not someone who throws it into the woods.

Not Frank Petít.

***

The Master Conversationalist set his copy of *The Heron* down on the table. He had read it at least fifty times since he left Greg's party the night before. He would probably read it another fifty times before he left this little cafe.

Café Gentrifique, as it were.

It was where The Master did all of his writing—reviews, reviews of reviews, the occasional act of plagiarism he kept locked in a drawer just for the thrill of it. But today, The Master had spent the entire morning putting quill to parchment on his Macbook Air to craft an entirely new brand of writing: the review of a review of a review of a review. Not even Cratchett had ventured into such meta frontier. He found the prospect titillating.

It was just about the only thing The Master Conversationalist found titillating at the moment. Indeed, one-upping Cratchett was the sole source of inspiration to spring The Master Conversationalist out of bed this morning. As a frequent partícipatór in the underground Brooklyn criticism community, he was accustomed to the occasional literary wrist-flick to the genitals, but he had never been on the receiving end of such a pointed spear to his manhood. Lucky for him, the Master didn't plan on taking this spear sitting down.

He took another sip of his verao morango and opened the Word document containing his response to Ada Cratchett. Having just re-read Cratchett's piece, now was the time to compare her work to his own.

The Master Conversationalist #437: Francois Petít reviews Ada Cratchett's Review of Francois Petít's Review of A.O. Scott's review of Remorse Considered

While I do not have a citrus allergy, let's assume that I was allergic to citrus. What would happen if I walked into some low hanging bananas? Nothing. Nothing would happen, because bananas are a non-citrus fruit.

The piece only got better from there. First, a brief tour of the history of pomology. Then a recap of The Master's critique of A.O. Scott's review, starting with Scott's failure to proffer a proper exposé on the yarn industry of nineteenth century Europe. Then a slight detour to discuss Cratchett's impotent accusation that The Master puts people in conversational prisons, followed by a detailed argument that his conversational *instrumentum navigationis* is much more like a sextant than a compass. Then, a very brief symposium on how playing catch is a child's first gateway into the opiate of organized sports, followed by the grand finale: a sniper shot to Cratchett's inflated ego with another one of The Master's classic closing paragraphs:

Ada Cratchett seems to think that Lukas Bauer's 1899 existential classic, Remorse Considered, is simply a film about a cat batting at a ball of yarn. Perhaps this is because, intellectually, Cleo is a ball of yarn. And I am the cat.

The Master Conversationalist smacked the table and took a long, victorious sip of his verao morango. When he was finished, he attached his response to an email addressed to the editor of *The Heron*, Jean-Claude Michel.

The Master Conversationalist slowly lowered one of his index fingers until it hovered over his mousepad. He stared at his finger. It was a good finger. Probably the envy of every pianist worldwide. But this finger wasn't destined for the ivory keys; at this moment, its purpose was simply to share his *singulari ingenio* with the world.

He hit submit.

All the air in his lungs left him. He slouched forward in his seat and looked out one of the big windows of Café Gentrifique. Per usual, the streets of Brooklyn were bustling with hipsters, but seeing these less-sophisticated urbanites did not fill The Master Conversationalist with the same smugness it usually did.

The Master turned back to his computer and opened *The Heron's* website. Jean-Claude Michel still hadn't published his piece. The Master hit refresh. Still nothing.

He went for another sip of his verao morango and, upon discovering the lack of beverage in his cup, ventured back to the counter to order another.

"What are we having?" said the barista. She smiled at him as she dried a dish with a towel. The Master Conversationalist scrutinized the woman. She wore the same non-uniform uniform as the other baristas at Café Gentrifique—serape, Hanfu shawl, kente cloth—but somehow, she wore it better, and The Master was surprised he had never noticed her before. And yet, on second thought, it was rare for him to notice peasant people.

"Another verao morango?" the peasant woman said.

"Please."

The peasant woman turned and started shaking a bag of coffee beans into a big machine with wooden gears and ropes on pulleys. When she was done, she set the bag on the counter and watched the steam rise. "So what are you working on?"

The Master paused. "What?"

"On your computer," she said, pointing. "I always see you in here typing."

"I'm writing criticism," The Master said, and when the peasant woman didn't respond, he added, "I shape culture."

"Oh," she said. "That's great."

"Yes," The Master Conversationalist said.

The peasant woman sighed contentedly. "I love learning about new cultures." And then, without offering him the courtesy of a warning: "Have you ever been to Portugal?"

The Master felt personally attacked. He knew very little about Portugal, and felt ill-equipped to dominate this peasant woman in a conversation about the country. "No, I've never been to Portugal," The Master said. "Why would you ever ask someone that?"

The peasant woman looked surprised. "I'm sorry," she said. "I just thought…you always order the verao morango. It's a very obscure Portuguese drink, isn't it? And not on our menu. Sorry."

The Master sensed in her tone that he had the upper hand. If he were so inclined, he could intellectually crush her. And yet, when his enormous brain tugged on its leash, he pulled back, demanding that it sit and stay. For now.

"I order the verao morango to put me in the right mindset for my writing," The Master said.

The peasant woman's eyes signalled some sort of delight. "I know exactly what you mean," she said. "Sometimes, I sit out on the patio here and drink a bica while I read about Portugal, and when the sun hits the honey locusts just right…" she kissed the tips of her fingers. "Belíssimo."

The Master could see that his coffee had finished brewing behind her, but the peasant woman was oblivious.

"I close my eyes and there I am!" she said, her hand stretched out in front of her. "Horseback riding the Alentejo! Eating polvo à la Lagareiro! Scrutinizing a Gregório Lopes pintura in the Museu Calouste Gulbenkian! You must feel the same way. Don't you, sir?"

The Master Conversationalist felt his left eyelid start to spasm. "Don't I what?"

"Don't you want to go to Portugal? Don't you want to sit out on the veranda of un café in Lisbon, watching the waves of the Atlantic crash into white sand while you...while you shape culture?"

The Master Conversationalist's mind tugged harder on its leash.

"Nietzche visited Portugal," he said.

The delight evaporated from the peasant woman's face. "Who?"

"At least, I think he visited Portugal."

"Who did?"

"Friedrich Nietzche," The Master Conversationalist said. "The philosopher."

"I don't think I'm familiar with him."

"That's okay," The Master said, "I can explain." The Master cracked his knuckles behind his back. "This morning, I was in the shower, letting the hot frothy water slap at my back like a liquid dominatrix. What I would give to be back in that water's pleasure dungeon right now. But, alas, in the corner of the shower, perched in a web on the cusp of the tub, what did I find? A spider. An eight-legged, ostracized object of social opprobrium. A sadistic subject of scorn. Poisonous? Probably. Disease-ridden? Indubitably. But wicked? Unclear. I could not say definitively that the spider deserved to be murdered via a swipe into the drain or a swift kick of a heel. But did it deserve to be helped? I didn't know. So, there I was, in the nude, watching the water from the showerhead ricochet off my chiseled form and cascade down dangerously close to the spider. I was at a crossroads, feeling equal urges to either kill the thing or simply turn off the water, hop out onto the bathroom tile, take a square of tissue paper, and delicately wrap up the monster to transport him to freedom outside. But the animal had other plans. It started climbing up the side of the wall, dodging the droplets of water raining down from above. Sure, I could have pelted the creature with a bar of soap, but what right did I have to play executioner with another being? The matter seemed settled. If I wasn't going to kill the thing, then I needed to save it. Those were my only two options. Right?"

The peasant woman said nothing.

"Wrong. Because right as I bent down to shut off the water, I noticed something. The spider—with its hairy legs dusted with miniature water droplets—looked unlike any spider I had ever seen. Was it a rare species? No. It was the same common house spider I had seen my entire life. But unlike all the other spiders, this spider was embracing its will to power. Somehow, during a simple, daily act of hygiene, I had stumbled upon the opportunity to witness the most important moment in this creature's extraordinarily short life. So I jumped out of the shower—but kept the water running—and sprinted downstairs to my parlor. I returned to my bathroom with my turntable and a vinyl record of Richard Strauss's Einleitung, oder Sonnenaufgang from his masterpiece Also Sprach Zarathustra—you may recall the track's notorious dun...dun...dun...DUN DUN from 2001: A Space Odyssey—and I turned the volume all the way up and positively blasted the track while I waved my hands, conducting—still in the nude—for my spider friend, who was a quarter of the way up the wall to becoming an Überspinne, and still well within the splash zone of the shower's deadly spray. The spider could have accepted its tiny nook of safety at the intersection of the wall and the rim of the tub, but this little spider wasn't going to settle for life's leftovers; it wanted power, and it wanted it—"

The Master Conversationalist's phone buzzed in his pocket. "One moment," he said to the peasant woman, and lifted his phone to his ear. "Francois Petít," The Master said.

It was his agent friend, Greg. "Frank, I have some news for you," Greg said.

The Master closed his eyes. "Greg, we talked about this."

"Right, sorry," Greg said. "Francois."

The Master looked over his shoulder at the peasant woman, who was blinking and looking around the room, as if reorienting herself to her surroundings. "This better be important," The Master said.

"It is," Greg said. "It's about your review."

The Master felt his sphincter clench. "My review of Ada Cratchett's review of my review of A.O. Scott's review of Remorse Considered?"

"That's the one," Greg said. "I was just reading it in *The Heron*,"

"*The Heron*?" The Master said. "So Jean-Claude Michel published it?"

Greg chuckled. "Oh he published it all right. But that's not why I'm calling. I'm calling because I'm shopping it around."

The Master grabbed onto the counter so hard, his fingernails dug into its splinters. "What do you mean 'shopping it around?'"

"I'm talking adaptations, Francois. Songs, movies, TV shows, comic books, vaudeville. Paramount already bought the film rights."

Spittle dripped down The Master's chin. "Paramount bought the film rights?"

"That's right, kiddo. And Disney's talking about turning it into a ride."

The Master Conversationalist was so surprised, he didn't even notice that this was the second time he had soiled a pair of trousers in Cafe Gentrifique. "I think...no...we need to...I need to…"

"We need to talk," Greg said. "Like ASAP. Things are moving quickly over here, Francois. I'm worried if you don't get your ass down to my office right now, the whole pizazz is going to peter out. You made a splash, buddy. Time to rub it all over your body before it drips down the drain."

The Master Conversationalist sprinted out the front door of Cafe Gentrifique, and then sprinted back inside to swipe his laptop into his satchel. On his second trip out the door, he heard the peasant woman calling after him.

"Your verao morango!" she said.

He paused in the doorway and looked back to see her holding the white ceramic cup high in the air. "Keep it," he said. "I won't need that where I'm going."

***

A weak mind once said that if you work hard every day, you'll be ready if your time comes. The Master Conversationalist, on the other hand, knew the truth: if you're brilliant and well-connected, eventually your agent friend will ask you to sign an eight-figure contract.

"I don't want to sell out," The Master Conversationalist said, pacing back and forth in Greg's penthouse office. "I didn't write The Master

Conversationalist #437 to sell T-shirts and coffee mugs."

"Of course, of course," Greg said, crossing out an entire page of the contract with a red pen. "We'll stick to the highbrow merchandise."

The Master paused in front of Greg's desk and stared down at him. "I want all the merchandise cut from the contract."

Greg looked up like a beached tilapia, gasping for another droplet of The Master's genius water. The parasite. "All of it?"

"All of it."

Greg began shuffling papers aggressively. "Just so you know, an artist in Buenos Aires has already started mocking up some sketches of you and Cratchett for some very tasteful action figures."

The Master swiped the papers out of Greg's hands and watched them scatter onto the floor. "Burn it, Greg."

Greg swallowed. He stammered gibberish for a few seconds before pausing to collect himself. "You're still open to the other things, right?"

The Master lingered for a moment before making haste for the opposite end of the room. With his hands clasped behind his back, The Master looked out the floor-to-ceiling window at the droppings of Brooklyn across the water.

"You at least want some movies to be made, correct?" Greg said. "And TV shows? Anime? Perhaps some novelizations of your piece? Francois?"

The Master ignored him. From his vantage point in Greg's Manhattan office, The Master could see the last vestiges of an ancient pier near the Williamsburg bridge. These days, all that was left of the pier was a bunch of wooden pillars poking out of the water. They were all lined up in perfect, obedient rows, all the same dark rust color, all in the same state of decay.

"Francois," Greg said, his voice growing more desperate with every word, "allow me to at least pitch you the plot of a potential buddy cop movie based on your review. It's being written by one of Hollywood's hottest new screenwriters, Buster Van Damm. Okay? You will be played by Timothée Chalamet, and your sidekick, a non-citrus fruit, will be played by Jack Black. Now, I know that in TMC #437, you originally referenced a banana, but I hope you'll allow the screenwriter the artistic license to replace it with a plantain."

Without looking back, The Master raised one of his pianist fingers to silence Greg. "Number Four-Thirty-Seven is not a buddy cop film," The Master said. He could hear Greg whimper a little behind him. "It is not," The Master said, pausing to prepare his lips to enunciate with sufficient pop, "a product."

"Francois," Greg whispered.

The Master raised a finger on his other hand to silence Greg once more. "I think we both agree that TMC #437 is a once-in-a-millenium work of art."

"Correct."

"In terms of influence, potentially on-par with most of the world's major religions."

"Don't be modest."

"What I'm afraid of is not that we'll commoditize my masterpiece. Nor am I afraid that we will oversaturate the market with my brilliance. No. What I'm afraid of is that we'll get so distracted by our efforts to commercialize my magnum opus, we'll miss the opportunity to solidify its place in permanent history."

Greg started to get up from his chair.

The Master raised both fingers high above his head. "Stay seated," The Master said.

Greg creaked back into his catcher's mitt of a recliner. "How do we—um—solidify your place—"

"When you light a match," The Master said, "who do you think of?"

Greg stammered. "A match, sir?"

"When you turn on the stove, who do you think of?" The Master could feel Greg's baffled expression behind him. "When you drive out to the Hamptons with a handful of friends, dig a pit in the sand, and throw a couple logs on top of a Duraflame doused in lighter fluid, who do you think of right before you toss your lit cigarette chode onto this ticking time bomb of your own creation?"

Greg's eyes widened. "Fire."

"Right, but who invented fire?" The Master said, turning around. He crept slowly toward Greg, pitiful Greg, pitiful Greg who would one day be dead, buried, forgotten, and lucky to provide the nutrients for a dandelion. "You don't remember who invented fire, do you?"

Greg shook his head.

"But you do at least find it a little curious that the creator of humanity's second greatest accomplishment was completely forgotten, don't you?"

Greg looked up at The Master towering over him. He shrugged. "It's a little odd."

"Well, do you know what this anonymous inventor's genius creation was missing?" The Master said, leaning in until he was close enough to bite Greg's nose.

Greg shook his head, closing his eyes to block out The Master's hot breath.

The Master pulled back, tapped his foot, snapped his fingers, and sang:

Tile floor, wood floor, bamboo, and laminate.
Carpet, cork, marble, vinyl, rubber, and ceramic—HEY!
Foam, terracotta, porcelain, and linoleum.
You'll meet all your floor needs at Flo's Floor Emporium!

The Master waited for Greg to open his eyes and lower his hands from their defensive posture in front of his face. "Have you heard that before?" The Master said.

Greg nodded. "I hear it on the radio sometimes."

"Does it get stuck in your head?"

"Yes."

"Song has a powerful effect on the human psyche."

"You want to turn your review into a jingle?"

The Master reached across Greg's desk and gently placed his hands on Greg's shoulders. "I want to turn it into a Broadway musical."

***

One Year Later

With his putter in one hand, A.O. Scott squatted down behind his ball and scrutinized the putt ahead of him. The green was dry and well groomed, with a slight left-to-right decline. No more than half an inch. He'd take that baby straight on if it weren't for the breeze from the northeast. Two knots. And chilly. Maybe a touch under forty-six degrees.

He stood up and shimmied into his stance. Out of principle, he did not take practice swings. He tapped his ball and watched it roll. It paused at the rim of the cup, taunting him.

"It's actually quite a scrumptious little production," said Charles Isherwood behind him.

A.O. massaged his forehead. "I told you not to talk during my backswing."

Charles looked offended. "I didn't."

"Yeah but you did when I was driving off the ninth tee and I'm still thinking about it."

Charles rolled his eyes. "A.O. you must relax. And just pick up your ball for God's sake. I'll give it to you."

"No," A.O. said. He shimmied into his stance again and tapped the ball. It rolled around the edge of the rim and came to a stop a few yards past the hole. A.O. covered his eyes. "I'm losing it, Chuck."

"We still have seven holes left."

"I mean I'm losing my mind." A.O. shimmied into his stance a third time. "I can't eat. I can't sleep." He tapped his ball past the hole. He looked at it longingly as it rolled down the backside of the green. "I have hemorrhoids," he whispered.

"There are creams for that."

"I've tried every cream, Chuck!" A.O. said, hurling his putter. He didn't flinch when it careened off the side of his golf cart. "But the bastards keep coming back. Big sacs between my cheeks. I had to get a standing desk. And a bidet, but that didn't do a damn thing. I thought a Japanese toilet would solve the problem—which it did—but only for a week, and now I've got to sit down on this little inflatable thing just to have dinner with my family."

"How do you like the heated seat?"

"The what?"

"On the Japanese toilet."

A.O. Scott glared at him.

Charles Isherwood pursed his lips. He sighed. "A.O., just see the musical."

"No," A.O. said, pouting.

They climbed into the cart and started driving.

"I think you'll find it quite flattering," Charles said. "Daniel Craig has perfected all of your little mannerisms."

A.O. Scott stopped licking his lips. "Is it flattering when Daniel Craig dresses up as an orange and gets twirled around on a juicer?"

"A.O., that is one song," Charles said. "It's a four-hour long production. Your character goes through quite a transformation."

"I'm a fruit!" A.O. screamed. "I'm a fruit the whole time!"

Charles Isherwood pulled the golf cart over on the side of the narrow path. He turned in his seat to face A.O. "In the beginning, you're a foreman in a nineteenth century Austrian yarn factory. Now, do you spend most of acts two through four as an orange? Yes. But during the Salvador Dalí sequence, you're Hans Gruber. And by the time Ada Cratchett dies in a sledding accident in the Citizen Kane scene in the seventh act, you have already become a ball of yarn that Francois Petít chucks into the woods. But this is all news to you, A.O., isn't it? Because you haven't even seen the damn thing."

A.O. Scott stared straight ahead, fixating on a particularly brilliant green knoll. In a nearby oak tree, he could hear a warbler singing a pleasant song—slightly out of key, and lacking the emotional depth of the Manhattan songbirds to which he was accustomed, but a pleasant song nonetheless. He swallowed. "I tried to make a musical once." Saying this aloud surprised even him.

"When?"

"At Harvard," A.O. Scott said softly.

"What was it called?"

"It was called...it was called Diesel." A.O. Scott looked off into the distance. He shut his eyes tight and waved his hands frantically. "It was stupid. I'm sorry. Let's go to the next hole."

"No, no," Charles said. He turned the key in the ignition to shut off the golf cart. "What was it about?"

A.O. Scott looked up at the plastic roof above him. "It was about these, like, rival architect biker gangs."

"Go on."

"Well, okay, so, there's this gang called the Flying Buttresses, who are hell-bent on erecting gothic cathedrals everywhere they can get a building permit. And that's all fine and dandy until Cyclops, the heir apparent of the FBs, falls in love with Charlene, the daughter of the ringleader of the Linear Sunbursts, this super rebellious group of art deco fanatics."

Charles Isherwood nodded as he watched a plaid-panted golfer shank his ball into a pond. "Okay," he said.

"You don't like it," A.O. said.

"No, no, I do," Charles said. "It sounds great." He squinted. "I'm just not sure if I understand, you know, like, why the architects are..."

"In biker gangs?"

"Yeah."

A.O. folded his arms and looked away. "You sound just like my professors."

"A.O…"

A.O. Scott started slapping the dashboard of the golf cart emphatically. "It's a story about forbidden love, conflicting aesthetic tastes, and the bond of the open road. How do you get all three of those things if the architects aren't in biker gangs? Tell me, Charles."

"I'm sorry."

"It's Westside Story meets The Fountainhead meets Harley Davidson and the Marlboro Man."

"It sounds wonderful, A.O."

A.O. Scott rubbed his goatee and shook his head as he looked down at his golf shoes. "It was wonderful. Was."

"What happened to it?"

"I burned it."

"You did?"

"All four-hundred pages." A.O. Scott picked up his scorecard, pretended to read it for a moment, and then tossed it into his cup holder. "The whole time I watched it burn, I thought, 'I will never feel this way again. From now on, I will be the one doing the criticizing. I will be the one in control. From here on out, I will tell the world what I think about it, and never the other way around.'" A.O. Scott looked Charles Isherwood in the eye. "And ever since then, I have lived my life according to one core principle: my ears are closed and my mouth is open."

Charles took a cigarillo out of his breast pocket and lit it. "I'm sorry to hear that, A.O."

A.O. shrugged. "It worked marvelously for decades." He looked away.

"Then Francois Petít came along..."

Charles blew smoke out of the corner of his mouth. "I meant I'm sorry you burned Diesel."

A.O. looked back at him. "Why?"

Charles took another drag from his skinny pencil of tobacco. "When I was at Stanford, I wrote a musical called A Taste of Murder. It's the story of Phillipe, an art philosopher with an impeccable eye for beauty. He's also an assassin who travels back in time to kill the creators of the Chrysler PT Cruiser." Charles flicked his cigarillo and watched the sparks fly as it hit the pavement. "I showed it to every faculty member in the Stanford theater department."

"And?"

Charles shook his head.

"Did you burn it?"

"The entire six-hundred-page manuscript." He looked at A.O. pensively. "But I wish I hadn't."

A.O. was taken aback. "Really?"

"Really." Charles lit another cigarillo. A layer of smoke rose in front of his face. "If I still had it—I don't know—maybe I would flip through it and cringe. But, maybe I would find a little piece of myself in that story—a piece I don't remember, or never fully recognized. And maybe I could take that little piece of myself and share it with someone else. And maybe they would say, 'I too sometimes want to go back in time and murder the creators of repulsive yet commercially successful products.' And that little connection—that tiny little connection—would be more fulfilling than my entire career as a critic."

A.O. Scott watched as the plaid-panted golfer on the eleventh fairway bent down to retrieve his ball from the pond and fell face-first into the water. "So this kid is the real deal, huh?"

Charles Isherwood nodded. "It's the best musical I've ever seen, A.O."

A.O. looked skeptical. "Better than The Phantom of the Opera?"

"Significantly."

"Better than Hamilton?"

"You better believe it."

"Better than Annie?"

Charles Isherwood scoffed. "*Francois Petít reviews Ada Cratchett's Review of Francois Petít's Review of A.O. Scott's review of Remorse Considered - The Musical* blows that little orphan's ass right out of the water."

A.O. Scott nodded reluctantly. He could see the plaid-panted golfer had already made it back on shore, and was lining up his next shot. "This Francois Petít must really be something."

"He is the chosen one," Charles Isherwood said, blowing smoke. "A master of both form and function." He turned the key on the golf cart and accelerated off the shoulder. "We better get to the next hole," Charles said, gesturing with his cigarillo to the plaid-panted golfer. "If this d-bag catches up, he might try to play with us."

***

The Master Conversationalist took another nip of bourbon before returning his flask to the velvet cupholder in his box seat in the Gershwin theater. He coughed as the whiskey went down his throat. He had assumed that, once he reached this level of success, the liquor would no longer burn, but even the most expensive bourbon still left behind a little tingling on the tongue. He leaned over the balcony to get one last look at the crowd. Another sold out show. The Master sat back and waited for the sense of accomplishment to wash over him, but he found himself feeling as numb as the tip of his tongue.

A few minutes later, the closing song Conscientiam Considerandum was in its closing verse. As Benedict Cumberbatch sang the song's last line, he, with the help of some stagehands dressed in black bodysuits, lifted up Daniel Craig, who was, as always, giving a spectacular performance as a ball of yarn, and chucked him into the woods. The Gershwin theater's 1,900 patrons exploded into thunderous applause, and the curtain snapped shut on the stage. As he did every night, The Master disappeared from his box before the lights came up.

The Master shook his flask as he walked down the hallway. Empty. The Master felt drunk, quite possibly even drunk enough to follow through with his plan. The Master's executive assistant, Randall, had informed him that A.O. Scott was in the audience for tonight's show, and The Master had spent the entire performance planning precisely what he would say to him.

The Master's first inclination had been to call out Mr. Scott at the very exclusive after-party with some of New York's most esteemed intellectuals. In front of everyone, The Master would propose a toast to Mr. Scott, and then deliver a series of bitingly backhanded compliments to the famed critic and his work.

Your first hit on Broadway, A.O. If I had known you were coming, I would have asked the stagehands to spin the orange on the juicer for another few rotations.

But if A.O. didn't know he was being insulted, he might take the bitingly backhanded compliments as actual compliments, and then A.O. would live the rest of his life thinking that he had inspired the greatest Broadway musical of all time.

So it might be more prudent to just insult A.O. to his face. It wouldn't be hard. The Master would simply inform A.O. that The Master knew far more Latin phrases than he did, that The Master had better taste in films, and that, while A.O. Scott was an accomplished film critic, The Master was the auteur of a global musical phenomenon.

But halfway through the fifth act, The Master started to have a change of heart, and by the start of the seventh, he no longer thought it appealing to let his conversational guillotine fall on A.O. Scott's neck after all. Subtlety was at the heart of conversational domination, and going against such a principle would insult everything The Master held dear. So, by the time Benedict Cumberbatch tossed Daniel Craig into the forest, The Master had already made up his mind. He would engage A.O. Scott in a long, private chat, and deliver him a slow death via a thousand conversational papercuts: small, incredibly petty little pricks to A.O. Scott's ego until it leaked out all of its life force and hung as limp as an overripe plantain.

The Master rushed down the steps that led backstage. He felt a little rush in his chest, the first sign of vitality in his numb soul in months. The feeling continued as he made his way to the press room where a few dozen critics, celebrities, and producers mingled while waiters walked around with trays of wine and hors d'oeuvres. By the time The Master opened the door and joined the buzz, the thrill he was feeling had reached its apex; when he spotted A.O. Scott across the room, gravity seemed to take hold of the giddy feeling in his chest, bringing it spiraling back to earth.

A.O. Scott, Critic At Large, was standing alone, nervously eating a shrimp, his eyes darting side-to-side. When he was finished with the shrimp, he held the little tail shell close to his chest and looked around desperately for a waiter with a tray. Unable to find one, A.O. checked to see if anyone was watching him and, unaware of The Master's hawk-like gaze, quickly deposited the little shrimp tail into his blazer's breast pocket. He was sweating profusely, and took out a little white hankie to dab at his forehead.

This was, The Master decided, not a man who required further diminution. But if The Master wasn't going to conversationally draw and quarter this critic, he wasn't sure if there was any point in talking to him. The Master's entire life felt as if it had led up to this very moment, but the moment was no match for how he had imagined it; A.O. Scott, Critic At Large, was not so large a critic after all.

So, then what? The Master wondered. Should he say hello to A.O. Scott? Ask him how his day was going? Thank him for coming to the show? Toss a ball into A.O. Scott's court?

The prospect was foreign to The Master. And it could lead to dangerous things. What if A.O. Scott wanted to talk about himself?

The Master turned on his heel, tipped his head back, and laughed at the Gershwin's dome ceiling as he walked out the door.

Sure, the two men were both critics, but other than that, what on earth did The Master Conversationalist have in common with A.O. Scott?

***

When The Master Conversationalist left the Gershwin, he waved off his driver, and instead walked the two blocks to his $30 million penthouse apartment. His wife, Cordelia, was playing the double contrabass flute when he walked in.

"Francois!" she said, setting aside her flute cannons. She ran across their living room to greet him. "I'm sorry I wasn't able to make it to tonight's show. I had to practice for the film scoring session tomorrow."

"What film?" The Master asked.

Cordelia looked puzzled. The Master realized it was the first time he had asked her a question since asking for her hand in marriage.

"I'm sorry?" she said.

"You said you were helping score a film," The Master said.

Cordelia laughed haughtily and flicked her wrist. "It's just a silly little Lord of the Rings spinoff called The Orcs or something. Tells the same story from the orcs' side. You would find it so incredibly mainstream. But enough about me!" She pulled up one of the stools at the counter and took a seat. "Tell me about your show."

The Master Conversationalist hung up his jacket. "It was just like all the others."

"Did Helena Bonham Carter use your notes?"

The Master shrugged. "She's trying, but she still hasn't perfected Cratchett's slithering walk."

Cordelia rested her chin on her hands. "That is so fascinating. I cannot wait to see it again with you."

"That's okay. You've seen it enough times," The Master said. He spun around and poured himself a glass of vodka.

"Francois..." Cordelia whispered. "Is everything all right?"

The Master's hand shook as he raised the glass to his lips. "I don't know," he said, and emptied the vodka down his throat. He brought the glass down hard on the counter. "Something happened today." He leaned against the fridge and stared at the counter as if it were several kilometers away.

"Francois," Cordelia said, her voice but a hint of a whisper on a windy day.

"Before the show," The Master said softly, "Bennie Cumberbatch invited me to do whippets and watch cartoons in his dressing room." He sighed. "So we go down there and get started, and I'm being my usual charming self: telling stories, lecturing, doing my damndest to educate Bennie about culture and the ways of the world. And then, Bennie turns on that one episode of the animated version of Fraggle Rock—you know, the one where Red and Mokey end up in the land of the Gorgs, and Wembley goes into space and has that moment where he's in a total daze?"

Cordelia opened her mouth and then closed it again.

"You can talk," The Master said.

"I was just going to say, it was a Wemblatonic fit, wasn't it?"

"That's right," The Master said. He poured himself another glass of vodka. "When Wembley went into his Wemblatonic fit..." The Master downed the vodka and tapped his chest. "...I felt as if I were going into a Wemblatonic fit too. Now, granted, Bennie had just stuck two tubes of nitrous up my nostrils, but for a moment, I couldn't..."

Cordelia nodded encouragingly.

The Master looked out the window at the end of his living room, thirty meters away. "...I couldn't speak," The Master said.

Cordelia inhaled sharply.

"I was a mute," The Master said. "A silent buffoon struck dumb by the force of Cumberbatch quality gas." The Master took two more shots of vodka and wiped his mouth with his sleeve. "For three minutes, all I could do was listen to Benedict Cumberbatch tell me this ridiculous story about how he backpacked the Pyrenees."

Cordelia gasped.

"It gets worse," The Master said. "First he's in the Pyrenees, then he's in Andorra, then Zaragoza, and then Madrid. Next thing I know, he's crossed the entire Spanish countryside, and he's entering El Parque Natural da Serra de São Mamede..."

Cordelia was leaning so far forward, her chinchilla collar was pressed against the granite countertop.

"And then..." The Master's voice trailed off. He frowned at the floor and shook his head. "And then..." The Master felt his knees start to buckle. He held onto the counter for balance.

"Francois!"

"I have to go," The Master said. He made for the door, but Cordelia caught him by the coat rack.

"Why don't you lie down?" she said.

"I have to go." The Master said. He shrugged her off and started putting on his coat.

"Francois!" Cordelia said. "We'll sit by the fire, and I can just listen!"

The Master bolted out of his apartment and ran down the hallway while Cordelia shouted behind him. Even when he was in the elevator, he could still hear her screaming, begging for a hot cup of tea and a monologue from The Master. It wasn't until he was several floors below his own that the sound of her voice dissolved into the percussive diddly of the elevator's smooth jazz. A saxophone called out, a piano responded, a bass thumped a little current under their bridge, and the elevator dinged as it reached the ground floor.

***

The wind whipped through the folds of The Master Conversationalist's scarf as he made his way to the 50th Street Subway. On each of the three trains he took to get to Brooklyn, The Master listened to at least one person screaming obscenities at another in a corner of the boxcar. Each time, The Master let them speak, saying nothing in return.

The Master got off the M train at Marcy Avenue in Williamsburg. He walked down tree-lined streets with brownstone homes where he could see families sitting down for dinner. At the edge of one of these neighborhoods, in between a dairy-free ice cream shop and an artisan cheese store, was Cafe Gentrifique. The Master opened the door.

Inside, it was just how he remembered it: modern yet vintage, woody with nutmeg notes, and a little damp. And behind the counter: the same barista he remembered from so long ago. He approached a little cautiously, and then, when he caught her eye, he leaned an elbow against the driftwood counter.

"I'll take a verao morango," he said, smiling at her as if he were reciting an inside joke that only they shared.

The barista looked confused, but she got to work on his coffee nonetheless, yanking on ropes, pouring strawberries into a hand-crank food processor, and shredding individual coffee beans with a potato peeler.

As he watched her work, the Master couldn't help but picture his future with this woman: holding hands as they ran along some unknown shore, looking out at the water from a hotel balcony, walking around one of those coastal cities in Portugal where every house had a bright red roof and bleach white walls. The Master didn't know the names of any of these cities, but the barista could teach him. She could teach him so many things, like how to give their future son a proper Portuguese name. The master was thinking Benedito, but he was open to Bonifacio, or anything. There were so many Portuguese names, probably. All he had to do was ask this person in front of him, this wonderful human being, his future wife—"

"What is your name?" The Master said.

"Jane," the barista said. Jane brought him his verao morango and set it on the counter.

"Did you ever go to Portugal, Jane?" The Master said.

Jane's eyebrows lowered three-eighths of a centimeter. "Yeah." She returned to the coffee machine, pressed a button, and said over her shoulder, "How did you know that?"

The Master swirled his verao morango in his cup. "Do you not remember me?"

Jane squinted at The Master.

"I used to come in here and write my reviews," The Master said. "You know, shape culture."

"Oh right!" Jane said. "Welcome back." And then, as another moment passed by, her memory seemed to return to her. She pointed at him. "Nietzche, right?"

The Master felt his chest swell with pride. "That's right."

"The überspinne in the shower."

"Well, I was but a humble witness—"

"You know, I did a little reading on your friend."

The Master lowered his verao morango from its lipward trajectory. "You read Nietzche?" The Master felt his heart racing. Bartolomeu, he thought. They could name their future son Bartolomeu.

"I did," Jane said, wiping down the counter with a rag. "Thus Spoke Zarathustra."

"Ah, yes," The Master said. "From his own mouth: his magnum opus. But if you ask me, I'm more inclined toward The Wanderer and His Shadow, or even Neitzche Contra Wagner. I find the latter especially riveting because you can really start to see the nascent stages of madness start to creep—" The Master paused. He watched Jane wipe down the counter. "But what do you think?"

Jane hung up the rag on a nail hammered into the wall. She shrugged. "I think if I were an übermensch—or, as I would say, a superfrau—I think my superpower of choice would be to have the chance to see myself exactly as other people see me." Jane took a broom from a nearby closet and began sweeping the floor.

The Master could already feel words churning in his stomach like a nausea he could not repress. "I think you may have read a faulty translation—" The Master Conversationalist began, but he interrupted himself with a long sip of verao morango. When he was done, he frowned and looked at the cup. "This verao morango," he said, choosing his words carefully. "It tastes different."

Jane stopped sweeping and leaned on her broom. "I have to admit, I don't know how to make a verao morango. Never did." She continued sweeping. "To be honest, I've never even heard of it. I tried looking it up, but I don't think it's a real drink."

The Master felt as if he could see his future fading before his eyes. Benedito, Bonifacio, Bartolomeu, all slipping away like sand through his fingers.

"I've just been throwing random crap in the coffee machine," Jane said. "The last time I made one of those things for you, I threw an entire plum in the grinder. You'd think an industrial-strength machine could handle it, but I was scraping pit chunks out of the gears until like six in the morning."

"Do you want to…" The Master Conversationalist began. He

swallowed. "Would you allow me to make you dinner sometime?" He scratched the back of his head. "I could fashion us some duck pâté en croûte. You could give me your take on superfrau."

Jane stopped sweeping. The blank look in her eyes told The Master all he needed to know. She took a ring out of her pocket. "I'm sorry," she said.

The Master held on to the counter to support himself. "When you went to Portugal," he said, finally, "you went with him, didn't you?"

She nodded.

"Is his name Benedict Cumberbatch?"

She shook her head. "His name is Carl."

The Master nodded and went for the door.

"Wait!" Jane said. When The Master turned, he saw her holding his verao morango. He realized he must have left it on the counter. "I made this one with strawberries," Jane said.

The Master held the cold brass knob of the front door in his hand. "So?" he said.

She shrugged. "It may be a made-up drink," she said, offering him the cup. "But this one has a little truth in it."

***

Outside, the verao morango in the Master's hand was but a small orb of warmth in an otherwise cold world. Not even his panda fur scarf or shearling kimono could insulate him from the frosty air as he trekked back to the subway station. By the time he felt the first raindrops on the tip of his nose, the little flicker of comfort from his coffee had long since been extinguished.

The Master lengthened his stride, cursing the rain that lashed down around him. As a young man, just a year earlier, he had assumed that success would protect him from every variety of discomfort and disappointment, but alas, misfortune, he realized, was an innovative parasite. Just when The Master believed he had developed immunity to misery itself, it evolved into an entirely new strain of heartbreak and disillusionment.

As he made his way, his curses of the rain turned into curses of his whole life: his career, his friendships, and even his wife who, bless her heart, couldn't possibly understand the torment of The Master's success. No one could. As the old saying went, *Auf der Höhe muss es einsam sein.* The Master, frigid and nearly catatonic, began to mutter the phrase under his breath.

Auf der Höhe muss es einsam sein.

It is lonely at the top.

Auf der Höhe muss es einsam sein.

But how could he have known?

Auf der Höhe muss es einsam sein

When he was a boy, he was a big fish in a small pond.

Auf der Höhe muss es einsam sein.

In high school, the captain of the debate team.

Auf der Höhe muss es einsam sein.

Sure, his graduating class only had eleven people, but Liam was a tremendous debater.

Auf der Höhe muss es einsam sein.

But no better than The Master himself.

Auf der Höhe muss es einsam sein.

No worse, either.

Auf der Höhe muss es einsam sein.

They were pretty much tied.

Auf der Höhe muss es einsam sein.

"*Sehr einsam*, indeed, Frank," said a voice.

The Master paused mid-stride and rolled back onto his heels. He looked to his right and immediately recognized the woman emerging from the shadows of the alley. "Cratchett," he said.

She smiled meekly, and The Master stepped back as if avoiding a striking cobra. Her radiant white smile was gone, replaced with a handful of yellow teeth. In the moment The Master took to collect himself, he noticed that much had changed about Ada Cratchett in the past year. The black dress she wore hung loosely on her gaunt shoulders, with a strip torn off at the hem that dragged on the ground. Her skin looked bare without any jewelry on. And when The Master looked down at her feet, he realized she was wearing only one boot.

"Ada," The Master said, his tone softening, "what happened?"

"Oh, you haven't heard?" Ada said. She grinned at him, smiling in spite of the sadness in her sunken eyes. "You're usually so well-read."

The Master could not bring himself to smile back. "What are you doing here?"

"Well, actually," Ada said, looking sheepishly at a puddle forming on the ground, "I came here to kill you."

The Master continued to clutch his kimono shut against his sternum. "Oh," he said.

"Yeah," she said. "I've kind of been stalking you for a while now." She raised her hands. "But I've already decided I'm not going to kill you. I promise. I already chucked the pistol into a trash can a few blocks back."

The Master nodded. "Into the woods, as it were."

"Oh, but…" Ada said, sticking her hand deep into her boot and coming out of it holding a very tiny pistol, "...I forgot I brought a backup one just in case I got cold feet." She pointed it at him for a moment before throwing it over her shoulder into the alley. It ricocheted off a brick wall and came to rest near a pile of garbage bags outside of a vegan pet food store.

"What made you change your mind?" The Master said, his eye still on the gun.

Ada sighed. "I realized that if I killed you, I would no longer have any purpose."

"And now?"

She chewed on her lip. "I guess I'm still trying to figure that out."

The Master took off his kimono and wrapped it around her shoulders.

"Thanks," she said.

"Thanks for saving my life."

Ada smiled as she wrapped the kimono over the top of her head and pulled it tightly around her shoulders. Within a few moments, she had stopped shivering, and The Master marveled at the fact that something which offered him so little warmth could provide someone else with so much.

"I take it you're not writing for *The Heron* anymore," The Master said.

Ada's yellow teeth made another appearance between her cracked lips. "It's been difficult to establish myself as a literary authority when my likeness is flapping her leathery wings on Broadway every night.

"Only for one song," The Master said.

"And I'm a Gorgon for another," Ada said. She stuck her hand out from the kimono just long enough to wave it dismissively. "Neither here nor there. I want to talk about you, Francois."

The Master could not tell if it was the walking or the fact that he was talking to someone wearing only one boot, but he felt warmer. "What do you want to know?"

"Was it everything you imagined?"

The Master looked down at Ada Cratchett's one boot. A sturdy, respectable rain boot with handles at the top. He wondered if she was storing any other weapons in it.

"No," The Master said. "No, it wasn't."

Ada nodded, and The Master could tell his words pleased her on some level, but on another level, they hurt her too.

"I do like the money," The Master said. "I bought a boat." He looked down at the pink spots on Ada's bare foot where her toenails used to be. "I can buy you another boot too. I bet I can find one just like it."

Ada looked away and wiped her eyes. "I have plenty of boots back home. Thigh highs, cowboys." She swung her arm in an arc. "The whole spectrum."

"And where do you live, Ada?"

Ada looked down the alley, and then, changing her mind, turned and pointed down the street. "In a brownstone down there." She rocked back and forth on her heels and held the kimono taut like suspenders. "I'm writing a Broadway musical myself. A grand production."

"What's it about?"

Ada stopped rocking. "It's about a woman who writes this thing, and it gets stolen, and she goes and kills the guy who turned it into a Broadway musical."

"Oh."

"I'm flexible about the ending."

The Master's phone started buzzing in his pocket. "Hold on one moment," he said to Ada, and answered it. It was Greg.

"Greg, I'm a little busy right now, can I call you back?"

Greg sounded as if he were in the shower, which he probably was. "Sure," he said. "How about I call you back and leave a message about A.O. Scott's review of your little play?"

The Master Conversationalist's toes curled in his Italian loafers. "What did he say?"

"He hated it."

"He did?"

"What did you expect?" Greg said. A scraping sound followed that The Master could only guess was Greg scratching his back with a giant brush. "I'm messing with you," Greg said. "He said he went home and cried like a baby over how beautiful it was."

The Master put his hand against his chest. "So he didn't mind the juicer scenes?"

"No. He said, and I quote, 'Citrus or non-citrus, Francois Petít can turn me into juice whenever he wants. My greatest honor would be if he turned me into a smoothie for the sequel.'"

The Master felt his smile flatten. "A sequel?"

Greg chuckled. "The big number two."

The Master picked at the panda fur on his scarf. "I'll have to think about it."

"You what?" Greg shouted over the running water.

"I'll have to think about it."

"Think about what?"

The Master paused. "I don't know if I have a sequel in me, Greg."

Greg turned off his shower. "What, are you out of your mind? This is A.O. Scott, Francois. Critic At Large. I get it if you don't want to sell printed T-shirts and G-strings, but when A.O. Scott says make him into a smoothie, you fire up the blender and start making me more hit songs."

"Goodbye, Greg," The Master said, and hung up before Greg could say another word. He smiled at Ada.

"I better go," she said and turned to walk down the alley, but The Master stopped her, partly because he didn't want to see her go, and partly because her tiny pistol was still visible next to a garbage bag overflowing with plant-based sausage sticks.

"Don't go," The Master said.

Ada's eyes were turning glassy. "You have your whole life ahead of you, Francois," she said. "I hope your sequel brings you whatever joy is missing from your life.

"It can't," The Master said. "But I know who can." He felt a salty, wet sensation on his lips that he had never before experienced. "Die Spitze muss nicht einsam sein," he said. "Will you help me write my sequel?"

Ada looked over her shoulder at her gun. When she looked back, she hung her head. "Can I think about it?"

The Master kept his eye on the gun. "Sure. How about I call my realtor, and we can talk about it in one of the houses around here."

Ada smiled. "I'd like that." She slipped her hand into Francois Petít's. Francois turned and led Ada down the street, careful to keep them both under the cover of an awning as often as he could. When the two Critics At Large were at the edge of a neighborhood, Ada paused on the sidewalk and let go of Francois' hand. "I have to confess," she said. "I wasn't totally fair in my review of your review of A.O. Scott's review of Remorse Considered."

Francois cocked his head to the side. "How so?"

"I don't always play catch either," she said. "Sometimes, I too slip up and chuck the ball into the woods."

Francois put his hand on Ada's shoulder. "That's okay," he said. "I'll be there to catch it."

THANK YOU FOR READING

If you can, please give this book an honest review on Amazon or Goodreads. Writing a review is the best way to support me as an indie author.

Also…

I have more books on the way. You can stay in the loop by joining my cult of funny at bakerhillbooks.com. I'll email you when I release a new short story collection or novel.

You can read a story from my upcoming collection on the next page.

WHAT'S THAT DOOR?

When I died and woke up in a tunnel, I thought, Oh come on. Really? I wanted nothingness. I had a hundred and four years of somethingness, and now? More somethingness.

No variety!

Behind me, complete darkness. Up ahead, a light.

Great, I thought. Everything has to be binary, even in death.

Then I saw a door to my left. The outline of it was really faint against the tunnel wall, but I could make out the frame and knob when I squinted. I brushed dust off the door. It was super dark in the tunnel, but I had pretty amazing night vision, so it was possible no one had even noticed the door in a long time—if ever.

I put my hand on the doorknob and paused. I looked toward the light. I imagined getting to see my parents and siblings again. But my neighbor Steve was definitely there, and he would for sure want to stop by my heaven house constantly. I looked toward the darkness, where I imagined a lot of my favorite golf buddies were. But there was also the eternal torture and hellfire thing.

I sighed. Maybe this side door contained the eternal nap I so desperately craved.

I opened it.

Bright lights.

A stage.

A studio audience.

A gameshow host with coiffed hair and a pinstripe suit.

"WELCOME BACK TO…" the host said.

"WHAT'S. THAT. DOOR," the studio audience shouted.

"The only game show disrupting the afterlife dichotomy."

I slammed the door shut. The sound echoed around the dark tunnel.

I looked back and forth between the light and the darkness.

Steve.

Eternal hellfire.

Family.

Golf.

Family.

But Steve.

Golf.

But the fire thing.

I opened the side door and walked onstage. The door slammed behind me with a permanent Your Choice Is Made kind of sound.

"Please welcome our latest contestant, Arthur!" the host said, reading a card. "A retired accountant from Omaha, Nebraska. He likes golf, birdwatching, and playing chess in the park. But let's see if the afterlife is going to checkmate him into eternal damnation! Spin the wheel, Arthur!"

The host gestured to a fifty-foot-tall wheel. It had three options: Heaven, Hell, and Back to Earth.

"Can we talk off-record?" I whispered to the host.

"Sure," the host whispered back.

"What is 'Back to Earth?'"

"Pretty self-explanatory. You go Back to Earth as a person our producers hand-picked for their entertainment value. Everything you do is filmed to entertain people in heaven and hell."

"Kind of like the Truman Show?"

"Legally, I can't say."

I looked up at the wheel. "Can I just go to hell?"

"No, you have to spin the wheel."

I sighed. "Fine." I spun it.

Back to Earth.

I was no longer on the game show.

I was on a different stage in front of a thousand hippies sitting cross-legged in a warehouse.

A woman sat in a chair next to me. She wore the same robes I was wearing, but she didn't have nearly as many bird patches and medals on her uniform.

"Master Arthur," the woman said. "What did you see?"

I looked around at the hippies staring at me earnestly.

"I'm sorry, what?" I said.

"When you went into your trance. Did you have any revelation you can share with us?"

"Oh, for crying out loud," I said. I looked heavenward. "Is this entertaining to you?" I looked hellward. "A cult? Really? Is this what you're all tuning in for?"

The woman looked out at the audience. "Master Arthur is still communicating with the gods."

I stood up and started dancing an Irish jig. "Is this what you wanted, you bastards?" I shouted at the ceiling. "Is this entertaining?"

"Master Arthur is still in his trance," the woman explained to the audience.

I stopped dancing to point at the bird patches on the woman's robes. "And what is this, anyway? A bird cult? What the fuck are these Girl Scout patches?"

The woman was still addressing the audience. "Master Arthur is now testing our faith—"

"Are you in on this shit?" I said to her. I looked out at the audience. "Are you all in on this?"

Most of the audience members looked at me curiously. Some looked on in horror.

I rubbed my eyes. "For god's sake. I just wanted to die. Can I die? Can you kill me? Is there a way out of this?"

"Master Arthur wants us all to drink the poison pomegranate juice," the woman said.

The audience stood up and started to shuffle toward a table along the wall. The table was filled with massive juice dispensers in the shape of exotic birds.

"No, no, no, no, no," I said, waving my hands frantically. "Stop!" I shouted. "I order you not to drink the juice!"

Everyone in the entire warehouse froze. The woman stared at me.

Just as she opened her mouth to interpret my statement, I jumped off the stage and sprinted toward the juice dispensers. I stuck my head underneath one of the faucets and unloaded a firehose-spray of juice into my mouth. I drank until I hit the ground, unconscious.

I woke up in a leather chair in a conference room. Across from me were five people in suits.

"Absolutely terrific," the woman directly across from me said. "Ratings were…" she looked at the guy next to her. "What were the ratings, Johnson?"

"Ten billion."

"Ten billion," the woman repeated. "An all-time high."

"Am I in…" I said, pointing up at the ceiling, and then down at the floor.

"Hell," the woman said.

"Hell. Gotcha," I said.

"But not permanently," the woman said. "This is just where our corporate office is. You were such an incredible guest on What's That Door, we want to give you your own show."

I paused. "Right, right, great. But is it cool if I just experience nothingness?"

The executives all looked at each other. "Nothingness?" the woman said.

"Yeah, yeah, just kind of blank emptiness, all dark, no consciousness. Any chance I could get that?"

The executives looked at each other again.

"Hold on one moment," the woman said.

All the executives scooted their chairs back so they could whisper in a circle. After a minute, they scooted back to the table.

"No," the woman said. "You have to have a show."

"What about heaven or hell? Can I choose one of those?"

"No. Show."

I sighed. "Any show?"

"Any show."

I made my choice.

When I came to, I was standing onstage in a cheap pinstripe suit. My hair was coiffed. A door opened at the edge of the stage. A man peeked in, looking scared.

"WHAT'S. THAT. DOOR," the studio audience yelled.

I ran for the door.

ACKNOWLEDGMENTS

Doc Rice, thank you for your help and encouragement while I wrote this book. Our conversations in the writers' room behind your garage helped shape The Ad Guys into the weird sing-a-long it is. You also had some excellent notes on The Big Orange Ghost, The Pudgy Boy, My Name is Jerry, The Master Conversationalist, and others. Most importantly, when I took good parts out of the book, you convinced me to put them back in. I know I can always count on you to tell me when something hits the mark, when it falls flat, and when it's absolutely essential for the story.

Ray, thank you for a one-of-a-kind cover. The buzz it generated for this book blew me away; people were ready to buy it before they'd read a single word. The cover is somehow both deeply unsettling but also cartoonishly tongue-in-cheek. You captured the jokingly cynical vibe of all the stories so well, especially The Ad Guys; the next time I see Jimmy Fallon interview a musician, I'm going to imagine him holding up The Ad Guys' album cover for the cameras.

Mom, it is no exaggeration to say I wouldn't be a writer if it weren't for you. I still remember when I was a kid, I wrote an essay you marked up with a red pen. I was frustrated, so I started arguing with you over every edit you suggested.

"If you want to get better," you told me, "you have to learn to take criticism."

You helped me learn to set my ego aside and focus on what I need to do to improve. Thank you.

Dad, your sense of humor has shaped my own since I was little. Listening to your jokes at the dinner table, watching comedies with you, hearing your stories of mischief from childhood—all of these treasured memories helped lay the foundation of what I find funny. So many moments in this book are little homages to the quirky side of life you introduced me to.

To my girlfriend and all my friends (especially Jim and Jim) who proofread this book, thank you for your love, help, support, and above all else, honesty all these years. Sometimes "This is not so good" is music to my ears, because it makes it all the more real when you say "Now this...this is okay."

Love,
Baker Hill

ABOUT THE AUTHOR

Baker Hill is an award-winning novelist, short story writer, and saxophonist who writes with a quill in a remote birdwatching tower in the Pacific Northwest. While his works are most accurately described as absurd comedies, they are also thought-provoking, genre-bending stories that will make your heart feel as if it's being hugged by a tiny gopher. Fans of George Saunders, Beth Lisick, Simon Rich, Lorrie Moore, and B.J. Novak will find Baker Hill's stories remarkably edible, even before covering them in peanut butter. Fans of laughing and gopher hugs will also find something to like in Mr. Hill's stories, and even if they fail to discover something redeemable, they can at least be comforted by the fact they helped feed a man stuck in a birdwatching tower. And pay for his supplies. His quill is running out of ink.

Is Baker still in the tower? Did he finally eat the pigeon delivering his ration of parchment and ink? Is he actually a vegan? Did Elon Musk really start the Backstreet Boys? Does Benedict Cumberbatch really do whippets and watch Fraggle Rock in his dressing room?

To find out, join Baker Hill's cult of funny at bakerhillbooks.com

Made in the USA
Monee, IL
12 February 2025